D0469796

GRANDPARENTING
THE AGONY AND THE ECSTASY

Grandparenting The Agony and the Ecstasy

Jay Kesler

Servant Publications
Ann Arbor, Michigan

Copyright © 1993 by Jay Kesler
All rights reserved.

Vine Books is an imprint of Servant Publications especially
designed to serve Evangelical Christians.

Published by Servant Publications
P.O. Box 8617
Ann Arbor, Michigan 48107

Cover design by Steve Eames

95 96 97 10 9 8 7 6 5 4 3 2

Printed in the United States of America
ISBN 0-89283-691-1

Library of Congress Cataloging-in-Publication Data

Kesler, Jay
   Grandparenting : the agony and the ecstasy/Jay Kesler.
      p. cm.
   ISBN 0-89283-691-1 : $8.99 (est.)
   1. Grandparents—Religious life. 2. Grandparenting—Religious
aspects—Christianity. 3. Child rearing—Religious aspects—
Christianity. 4. Grandparent and child. I. Title.
BV4528.5.K47 1993
248.8'4—dc20   93-15810

Contents

Introduction

1. We're All in This Together / 11
2. "In Today's World We Need..." / 19
3. Hands Off, Hands On / 29
4. Putting Down Roots / 45
5. Finding the Common Ground / 61
6. Generations of the Faithful / 85
7. The Spittin' Image / 101
8. Building Memories / 113
9. When Our Children Divorce / 125
10. When In-Laws Become Out-Laws / 147
11. Surrogate Grandparents / 157
12. Meaning through Mortality / 173
13. Providing Support / 185

Introduction

GRANDPARENTS HAVE ALWAYS played an important role in
providing stability and support to families. The Apostle
Paul begins his second epistle to Timothy by reminding
him of the background and heritage of his family—the
faith and character of his mother Eunice and his grandmother Lois. Paul encourages Timothy to imitate the
examples of these godly women, who lived devout lives in
the midst of a pagan society.

Sometimes we are tempted to assume that the modern
world is more complex than the first-century environment in which Timothy lived, that family life in biblical
times was less complicated. We don't know all the details
of young Timothy's life, but we do know that he was the
product of a mixed marriage—a Greek father and a
mother who was a believing Jew. Some scholars suspect
that Eunice might have been a single parent, perhaps due
to religious incompatibility. Paul, at least, does not
attempt to evoke memories of Timothy's father or refer to
his example.

And even beyond Timothy's individual situation, biblical
history reveals that the family structure of the first century
was at least as tension-filled and stressed as it is today.
Infidelity, abuse, incompatibility, and divorce plagued the

family structure. War, poverty, depression, epidemics, slavery, and exile threatened the stability of family life.

Young Timothy needed the strong spiritual roots provided by his mother and grandmother. And young people today, facing those same tensions, need godly parents and grandparents to help their own roots go deep so that they might withstand the winds and storms of everyday living.

To meet that need, God in his divine wisdom ordained that each child should have *six* adults to provide care and backup. In ancient times, because of disease and accident, life expectancy was short. Families were often broken up as fathers went off to war or mothers were sold into slavery. The involvement of the extended family, especially grandparents, was crucial to the survival of the children.

In a similar way in the United States, matriarchs in the black community often proved to be the social strength to enable family life to continue amid the havoc wreaked upon families by slavery. These grandparents, who gave their grandchildren a foundation of moral character, often persevered with the strength gleaned from prayer and deep faith in the ultimate justice of God.

As we draw to the close of the twentieth century, many families will face similar challenges—not because of slavery, but because of the breakdown of the moral and social fabric of society. In single-parent homes or families where both parents work, grandparents become increasingly important. In the past, war left hundreds of thousands of children in single-parent families, and in the majority of cases families closed ranks and provided love and support to make the best of difficult situations. This generation can do the same, especially if Christians understand that this is not only a social challenge, but a spiritual battle as well.

In the Scriptures, the family is the one consistent metaphor used by God to communicate his relationship to humankind. God is a heavenly father. We are God's children, and thus brothers and sisters. We are the family of God. Christ is the bridegroom; the church is his bride. We are the household of faith.

All these terms are understood within the context of family life. If families are lost, we also lose our ability to comprehend clearly our relationship with God. If family life is lost, faith is lost. By every measure from church attendance to the rate of illegitimate births, the moral and spiritual fabric of society shreds with the breakdown of family life.

In this important battle, we encourage a recommitment to Christian grandparenting. The whole weight of responsibility cannot rest on an individual set of grandparents or a single grandmother or grandfather, but we can "stand in the gap" in our particular situations.

This book will attempt to identify that unique position of grandparents in family life. As grandparents, we can do more than give our grandchildren fond memories. We can lay a solid foundation under their feet, offer them a sense of continuity with the past. And if we can interest them in the recent past as expressed by their grandparents, perhaps we can help them connect as well with the biblical narrative and with the God of history.

It is a grand challenge—and a grand idea.

We can make a difference... to our grandchildren, to the future, and to the kingdom of God.

ONE

We're All in This Together

Y EARS AGO, I was in Nairobi attending a Youth for Christ conference when a controversy developed between entrenched older leadership and aspiring young staff. It appeared to be a standoff, with neither side compromising.

At last an African man stood to his feet and told us this story:

Once there was a village in which all the young men had grown tired of living according to the old ways. They decided that the old men held no value, and they no longer wanted to live according to the regulations and restrictions of their fathers.

So the young men conspired to kill all their parents and take control of the village for themselves. All agreed except for one young boy who couldn't bring himself to kill his father. He built a little hut and hid his father in the jungle, brought food to him, and helped him survive.

One day when the young men were out hunting, the new leader of the village was surprised by a giant python. The serpent wrapped itself around the young chief, and the warriors could not figure out how to help their leader. If they shot arrows into the python, they might kill their leader as well.

At last the young boy ran into the jungle to ask his father's advice. The old man appeared with a young goat and held it up for the python to see. When the serpent realized that a more tender meal was being offered, it unwrapped itself from around the young warrior and devoured the goat instead.

The old African's point was well taken. Sometimes the younger generation loses out on the value and wisdom of their elders because they do not have eyes to see what the older generation can offer them.

We are all in this together, and we need to learn to benefit from each other's experiences.

❧

Sometimes the younger generation loses out on the value and wisdom of their elders because they do not have eyes to see what the older generation can offer them.

KILLING OFF THE OLD WAYS

You don't have to look far or have very good vision to see that the Western world is experiencing a cultural revolution that has touched every family in America. We have not physically killed our parents and grandparents, but we have, as a culture, redefined many of the rules so much that the ideas and values of the past are, for all practical purposes, dead.

Words like commitment, sacrifice, fidelity, discipline, and authority are out of fashion. Love is defined as an emotion rather than a decision, and the word is often used as a synonym for sex. In the world of television—both on and off the screen—love is seldom enduring, and usually self-serving.

Language is changing to accommodate this radical shift in values. Vocabulary that was once limited to smoke-filled bars and dark pool halls is now everyday slang among young people of both sexes. Some of the terms are simply crude or uncivil; others represent a deep reversal of sexual codes and moral standards; still others reflect the shifting values of society.

Even the few positive family images offered by the media reflect these radical changes. I remember my own mixed feelings when I first saw the movie, *On Golden Pond*. The film poignantly illustrates the relationship of older lovers and the feeling of grandparents toward their grandchildren. It is one of the finest films I have seen. But the gutter language included in the movie distracted me from the message. It didn't fit, and everyone I talked to who was over fifty agreed that the language was a distraction. Ironically, young people didn't seem to notice.

CULTURE CONNECTORS

Because the breakdown of societal values and the changes in society's mores are so subtle, grandparents can play an important role in stabilizing the lives of their grandchildren. They can become carriers of culture from one generation to the next, connecting links that keep society rooted in past values.

Grandparents have the opportunity to pass on the experience-based wisdom that is missing in the lives of many young people today. And perhaps most important of all, grandparents can serve as a spiritual catalyst to the younger generation, demonstrating for them the reality of life in Christ.

❧

Grandparents can become carriers of culture from one generation to the next, connecting links that keep society rooted in past values.

Christian faith has always been about commitment—not simply commitment to an idea, but commitment to a person, Jesus Christ, and to the incumbent values of Christian faith. Perhaps that is why Paul emphasized to Timothy the value of investigating and imitating the faith of his grandmother Lois and his mother Eunice. Grandparents can help young people identify what they can commit their lives to.

I personally had no contact with either of my grandmothers—both died before I was born. But my grandfathers instilled in me values and memories that can never be taken away.

My mother's father, Grandpa Campbell, was a blacksmith. He took me in his 1937 Hudson Teraplane from farm to farm, dairy to dairy, riding stable to riding stable, to watch him shoe horses. I turned the crank on the forge, saw the iron heat up in the white-hot coals, felt the steam rising from the cooling barrel, smelled the scent of hot iron and horseflesh.

I remember his muscular arms, and when I think of

him I see those same strong hands stroking the neck of a frightened animal, gentling him, settling him down. From my grandfather Campbell I learned about the strength that a good man can bring in times of trial and difficulty.

Grandpa Kesler had an even greater effect on my up-bringing. For hours I would sit in his lap while he sang lullabies to me in half-English/half-German phrases. I didn't understand all the words, but his presence brought comfort and sleep. Once when I was very small, I am told, he held me for ten hours when I had whooping cough. But mostly I remember sitting next to him as he drew pictures of barns and stables and told me about life on the farm. We lived in town, and our generation was very different, but his world became real to me because he took time to share it.

And every Sunday, without fail, Grandpa Kesler would put on his only suit and walk several blocks to church. He showed me that even strong, self-reliant men need to carve out time in their week to acknowledge their dependence on a stronger and more reliable God. His patient faithfulness and stability eventually reached his entire family.

Over the years I have worked with thousands of teenage boys who thought that faith was for women, that real men drank hard, swore hard, and womanized every chance they got. Perhaps if they had had a grandfather like Grandpa Kesler, they would have grown up with a much different image of manhood.

THE CLEAR PICTURE

I remember my grandfather's photo album—five inches thick, and filled with very old photographs, some of them tintypes from the Civil War period. I can still visualize pictures of people, identified and unidentified, who are part of my early childhood. Even now I sometimes look through that album for favorite pictures of relatives still living and those who have long since died.

And what strikes me most about those old photos is the realization that life hasn't really changed all that much. I look at the browned and faded pictures—a happy engaged couple standing beside a vintage automobile; a young man at the beach showing off his muscles; a group of softball players with fixed smiles, looking casual and healthy and strong. And I imagine I know something of these strangers; their attitudes and actions, captured on film, speak to me of the quality of their lives.

My wife Janie and I are now building photo albums that will no doubt be viewed in the same way by future generations. I hope these pictures will evoke memories of happiness and feelings of fondness for family life. I trust they will be the basis for the solidarity and acceptance that all families seek.

Our grandchildren look at the pictures of Janie and me in our dating days, at our wedding—with me ever so thin in a borrowed dinner jacket—and involved in other activities of our early lives together, and wonder if I ever was that free and fun and casual.

৵

But the needs of my grandchildren—to see me as I am, to know me—are important enough to drag me away from my adult preoccupations.

Sometimes I wonder myself. These days I feel rather like those old pictures of Richard Nixon walking on the beaches of San Clemente in a three-piece suit and black wing-tipped shoes. The photographers wanted him to have the common touch, and so did he. But his role—and perhaps his personality—demanded that pinstriped suit and wing-tips. In a similar way, the responsibilities of daily life sometimes threaten to rob me of my longed-for spontaneity.

But the needs of my grandchildren—to see me as I am, to know me—are important enough to drag me away from my adult preoccupations. I want to take off my shoes, loosen my tie, and run on the beach with my grandkids.

In a physical sense, those photos are important. I want my grandchildren to see the whole scope of my life, to look at me as a real person, a person who once was as young as they are. I want them to realize that I have struggled with the same issues they are dealing with, and have managed to survive the struggle. I want them to feel a sense of connectedness with the past—their past, their history—so that they will have a sense of direction about the future.

But more important than the physical photos are the spiritual photographs we pass on to our grandchildren—snapshots of God at work in our lives; candid photos of real people who exercised living faith in a real God.

When my grandchildren look at the photos of my youth, they see a person very different from who I am today. Sometimes they laugh; sometimes they are amazed at the differences. But I hope that the picture my life is developing for them is an accurate and true representation of who God is, a reflection of the kind of man or woman God is calling them to become.

The world is changing rapidly—too fast, perhaps, and in the wrong directions. Young people need something stable to hang *on* to—a culture connection, a sense of their own past, a hope for their own future.

Most of all, they need what grandparents can give them—a picture of the long-term faithfulness of God.

❧

*Young people need something stable
to hang on to—a culture connection,
a sense of their own past, a hope for their
own future. Most of all, they need what
grandparents can give them—a picture of
the long-term faithfulness of God.*

TWO

"In Today's World We Need..."

BECAUSE OF MY YEARS of experience in radio broadcasting with the program called "Family Forum," I receive thousands of letters each year—letters responding to the radio program, asking questions, seeking help. Probably half of those letters come from grandparents, and some of them relate heartbreaking stories about tragedy in their families.

In some cases the sadness is sudden and final and tragic beyond measure: stories of infidelity and divorce, of parents who test positive for HIV and children who are born with AIDS, of drug addiction, unwanted pregnancies, and abuse.

In other cases the letters relate unavoidable circumstances that disrupt the family: parents with cancer, heart attacks, strokes, and mental illness; babies born deformed or terminally ill; loved ones lost in automobile accidents or plane crashes.

Still other letters reveal struggles brought on by the influences of sin and society: materialism, mid-life crisis, the victimization of children.

Grandparents often feel helpless in the face of such immense pressure and struggle. They watch with a growing sense of desperation as their adult children strive to "have it all" and lose their sons and daughters in the process. They see how tension between the parents affects the children; how total commitment to job and success leaves little room for family. Yet they feel anachronistic if they make suggestions or voice their opinions. Times are different, they are told. They just don't understand.

So marriages break up, families fall apart, and custody battles rage. And as the dust rises around the crumbling ruins of the family, grandparents stand by not knowing how to help or what to do.

A PLACE TO BEGIN

When disaster strikes the family, many people don't realize that there is an underlying reason for the breakdown of society's structures. Human beings have limitations, and the experience of the ages has taught us about the importance of love and support, about the necessity for extended families and the need for God. Human beings need redemption—even, in some cases, remedial efforts to correct mistakes of the past.

The difficult issues facing modern families do not take God by surprise. God knew the problem was coming. That's why Jesus Christ was the "Lamb slain before the world began." Something has to be lost before it can be redeemed. God understands our lostness and specializes in finding us wherever we are and saving us. Fragmentation and pain have to come before reconciliation.

These biblical ideas of redemption, salvation, and reconciliation are not simply dead theological terms, but descriptions of God's gift to the human race. God has heard it all, and God stands ready to answer all those who call out for help.

Part of that answer for the family may lie in the wisdom and love of grandparents.

ॐ

The difficult issues facing modern families do not take God by surprise. God knew the problem was coming. That's why Jesus Christ was the "Lamb slain before the world began."

WHAT GRANDCHILDREN NEED

Almost invariably, the letters I receive from grandparents include a phrase like this: "In today's world, I think we need...." Despite the assumption that old people are not in touch with the so-called "real world," their insights and evaluations reflect that today's grandparents are, indeed, connected to reality—and they want to do something about it.

And what, according to these wise grandparents, do their grandchildren need?

1. They need security. "Four of our grandchildren have gone through divorce," one grandparent wrote. "I want them to feel loved in a place where there is no friction. We try to let them know that we still love both of their parents."

Children, even very small children, have a sense of that

security—or the lack of it. A teenager said: "I lived with my grandparents for years as a small child. I always loved their house. It represented security and someplace that I could always count on. Even the furniture was always in the same place."

2. They need time. "With both parents working hectic schedules," a concerned grandmother observed, "it's important for our grandchildren to know that we will make time for them if we possibly can."

A college student told me about his awareness of the importance of that availability to a child: "During my elementary school years my parents weren't available for me. They were divorced and my mother and father both lived out of state and I didn't see them often. My grandparents were the ones who took care of me and were always there when I needed them."

3. They need acceptance. "Our grandchildren's parents had to get married," another grandparent wrote. "The other grandparents never accept them like the other grandchildren. They play favorites. We're trying to figure out how to be real Christian grandparents and forgive as Christ has forgiven and help these kids not grow up with a stigma on their lives."

A letter from a student said, "Children need to be kept in touch in a divorced family…. I feel very blessed that we have kept the relationship open. It has been a blessing to us all. There is no place for negative feelings and severed relationships because of divorce. I would have been devastated to have been cut off from my grandmother, and I feel very strongly about keeping those ties tied."

4. They need love. A young woman wrote to me about her need for unconditional love: "My paternal grandfather and I were especially close. He was a very powerful man in our hometown and I was illegitimate at conception. He not only claimed me but let the entire town know he was proud of me. I was his princess and he gave me the first understanding I was to have of what unconditional love could be."

Even very small children can be profoundly affected by such love. One young man said: "I lived with my grandparents the first two and a half years of my life. Grandpa treated me special. He sang to me after supper and played his harmonica. He hugged me and was proud of me, and he also made me behave. He only had to look at me and I obeyed."

૨૭

Redemption always costs something.
Intervention is never cheap.

When I read letters like these, I see between the lines the tears, despair, pain, and tragedy of the lives they represent. But I also see intervention by caring grandparents, many of whom probably felt they were only doing what came naturally. I can imagine, however, that these loving grandparents postponed their own dreams, canceled vacations, disrupted their private lives, and spent their retirement incomes to be available to their grandchildren.

Redemption always costs something. Intervention is never cheap. Christians understand this truth in relationship to the cross, where Jesus gave his very life to intervene on our behalf to save us from the results of our own sinfulness.

Taking up your cross daily is not like hanging a piece of jewelry around your neck. It means sharing in the suffering of others.

Grandparents are sometimes called upon to make such sacrifices. But God's promise does not fail: "If you lose your life for my sake, you will find it."

FAITH FOR A LIFETIME

Our own journey of becoming grandparents was not fraught with all the tragedy and difficulty reflected in the letters I receive. But even when the transition to grandparenting comes naturally and joyfully, the changes can be a shock to the system.

Our first grandchild, Wesley, came as something of a shock to all of us. Our daughter Laurie and her husband Tom were attending a state university, where Tom was finishing his degree in marketing. They had agreed to postpone starting their family until they had finished school and paid off their education loans.

But little Wesley just wouldn't wait.

It was a good thing for Laurie and Tom—and for Janie and me—that babies aren't born immediately after conception. This pregnancy was not Plan A for Laurie and Tom, and we all needed the remaining months of the pregnancy to get used to the idea and get prepared.

After the initial adjustment, Laurie and Tom decided to make the best of it and began to look forward to parenthood. Laurie happily went down to a clinic close to the university for prenatal care and was immediately confronted by a doctor who began to criticize her for not coming in earlier. "I cannot abort this baby easily at this stage!" he said. "You've waited too long."

Abortion was the furthest thing from Laurie's mind, but the doctor had supposed that she was an unmarried college student who was pregnant out of wedlock and wouldn't want to keep the baby. Once she got over the shock of his assumption, the doctor bluntly gave her another bit of disturbing news: since conception had taken place while she was on the pill, there was a high chance that the baby would be deformed or retarded.

Laurie was devastated—both by the implication that it was "her fault" that the baby might be handicapped, and by the physician's brusque and tactless bedside manner.

We got a second opinion which somewhat alleviated Laurie's concerns, but that first doctor robbed Laurie of some of the joy of her pregnancy and instilled in her some lingering doubts and concerns.

Little Wesley was born completely healthy, and all our concerns were unfounded. And perhaps the struggle and fear in the months leading up to his birth have contributed to a bond between us that is very strong. Whatever the outcome, the experience of Wesley's birth showed me that sometimes, as grandparents, we have to step in and lend strength and faith to our children when they don't have it for themselves... whether we feel ready to be grandparents or not.

WHEN THINGS GO WRONG

All stories don't end as happily as ours. I remember a long night sitting in a coffee shop listening to a friend pour out a mixture of sorrow, fear, faith, and doubt. Their long-awaited first grandchild had been born with Down's Syndrome. I listened and empathized and tried to be a friend to him as he worked through his emotional responses to this crisis.

I gave him a copy of Dale Evans Rogers' book *Angel Unawares*, the story of her and Roy Rogers' experience with a Down's child. I also recommended Morris West's novel, *The Clowns of God*, which had given me some insights. He had read Philip Yancey's book, *Where Is God When It Hurts?* and together we struggled for strength and perspective, especially in adjusting personal aspirations to the circumstances at hand and, more profoundly, to the will of God.

When things go wrong, each family must adjust, and each grandparent must face the unique challenges of the situation. But in these circumstances, the faith of the grandparents can be a stabilizing factor for the entire family.

A challenge of a similar nature came to our own family with the birth of our daughter Terri's second child. Terri and Phil had one child, Luke, who had gone through serious surgery but came out fine. With their second pregnancy, they weren't expecting anything out of the ordinary.

Katelyn, however, had her own agenda. She came much sooner than planned.

At birth, Katelyn weighed three pounds, and within hours she was down to two pounds, eleven ounces. Until Katelyn came, I never knew how many "preemies" major hospitals have to deal with. There, amid twenty-five other tiny newborns, was a little incubator holding a very little person.

Her head was about the size of a billiard ball; her legs were smaller than my little finger. I knew that newborns are hardy little creatures, but I was afraid to pick her up... afraid of doing something wrong.

As I lifted my granddaughter in one hand and saw her minute, perfectly-formed fingers and toes and ears, I suddenly remembered all the academic discussions about abortion I had heard over the years. Seeing and holding this tiny little person, with her incredibly small fingernails and eyelashes and all the working parts, was a more profound case against abortion than any argument I had ever heard.

During the six weeks when Katelyn was confined to the preemie ward, we all banded together to encourage each other, learn what we needed to know, and bond with this tiny infant in the incubator. Now that Katelyn is two and a half, we watch her grow with a special sense of pride and thankfulness—both for God's protection and for our opportunity of supporting and encouraging her and her parents through our faith.

ह

When things go wrong,
the faith of the grandparents can be a
stabilizing factor for the entire family.

In today's world, grandchildren—and their parents—need the support of grandparents who have walked with God through adversity and struggle. They need to see what faith in God can do when times are difficult, what supernatural strength and endurance the Spirit gives in time of need.

Grandparents can be that for their grandchildren—a beacon of faith. As they offer time and security and acceptance and love to their grandchildren, they demonstrate by living example the availability and faithfulness of God.

ॐ

In today's world, grandchildren need to see what faith in God can do when times are difficult, what supernatural strength and endurance the Spirit gives in time of need.

THREE

Hands Off, Hands On

I'M NOT SURE ANYONE is ever really ready to be a grandparent. I remember meeting a woman at a family conference a few summers ago—a vital, lively woman who was attending the conference with her three small grandchildren and their parents.

After being around this family for a while, I began to observe a very interesting phenomenon: the children always called their grandmother by her given name, Karen—not Gram or Grandma, but Karen.

When I asked her about it, Karen told me that she didn't *feel* old enough to be a grandmother. She played golf, went to the country club, had a beautiful tan, dressed nicely, and was, in all ways, a modern, active woman. She wasn't ready to accept herself as a grandmother, so her grandchildren called her "Karen."

ટ્રે

*We cannot stop the passage of time...
we can merely learn to accept
our new roles graciously.*

We can joke all we like about the reality of mid-life crisis; about men buying sports cars and wearing gold neck chains and trying to look twenty years younger than they are; about women having face lifts and coloring their hair to push back the encroachment of the years. But the sad fact is, we cannot stop the passage of time... we can merely learn to accept our new roles graciously.

I think one of the reasons God ordered human life in generations is so that we who are aging can watch the younger ones grow up and fulfill their dreams. They push us on to new vistas and allow us the opportunity to search for the new roles we must play when we arrive at the autumn of our lives.

As we age, perhaps what we need more than anything is the grace of God to live each chapter of our lives without regret, to discover the charm and blessing each phase of life offers to us. We cannot relive the past. We live in the present. But the past serves as a prologue, preparing us for the calling of the present.

ન્જ

We cannot relive the past. We live in the present. But the past serves as a prologue, preparing us for the calling of the present.

HANDS OFF

We've had our shot at parenting. We've done the best we could, and our children are the product of our work. Even our failures provide experience that makes us wiser, more patient, and more forgiving. Now, as grandparents, we become a support to our children as they attempt the confusing and demanding task of parenting.

I believe one of the major roles of the grandparent is to be cheerleader—that is, to encourage our children in their own parenting. We have already given advice in the form of our own theory of parenting and our own conduct over their entire lifetimes. Now is the time for encouragement and support.

As I read letters sent to me from the radio program, "Family Forum," I am amazed at how many marriage problems relate to parental interference. Few, perhaps none, of these parents or in-laws intend to contribute to the divorce rate, yet they do. We need to realize that when our children have children, a change of strategy and tactics is in order. We need to keep our hands off.

꿍

We've had our shot at parenting. Now, as grandparents, we become a support to our children as they attempt the confusing and demanding task of parenting.

Once we have grandchildren, we need to do a great deal of listening, observing what they say when they visit our home. The temptation to interfere—even with a raised eyebrow—is great. But we can have a very powerful influence by saying, "What great parents you have! You're blessed to have a daddy like that," or "That was sure neat what your dad did! I think that was very special for him to take time on Saturday to take you all to the skating rink." Cheering on the parents as well as affirming what they do is a proactive contribution, both to your child's marriage and to your grandchildren's development.

Many young parents are insecure as a result of being bombarded with conflicting advice on parenting. The subject of discipline alone is one of the most confusing issues in our culture. Christian experts encourage consistent discipline, for example, but almost all the secular advice from professional psychologists and secular child experts discourages discipline of any kind.

Thus, our sons and daughters tend to be very tentative about their parenting because they don't want to do it wrong. When we see them do things right and when we see them making attempts to be good parents, words of affirmation and encouragement can be of great value. "You know, your mom and I are extremely proud of the way you are taking care of your family. We're really proud of the kind of family you're raising. And I've noticed the way you relate to each other as a couple. I think the kids see that and it has real value."

ॐ

Cheerleading for the parents as well as affirming what they do is a proactive contribution, both to your child's marriage and to your grandchildren's development.

A hands-off policy does not mean indifference. Affirmation is vitally important—all of us need approval from our parents, regardless of age. Many men confess that nearly all they do is an attempt to gain approval and a "well done" from their fathers. And women feel the same way. Many women give up on ever really pleasing their mothers and turn unconsciously toward their fathers, who are often more accepting of daughters.

Encouraging our children and helping them to feel secure at times of tentativeness and uncertainty can be an important role for grandparents. I have joked sometimes about my dad "living on my bedpost," watching and evaluating my every move. All my life I have done things to seek his approval; I am amazed that I am unable to escape this desire even though he's been dead for many years.

While we're still alive and our children are raising their families, spoken words of encouragement have great power. Affirming the choices they've made—choices about family priorities, choices about their use of money, affirming every possible thing we see that has value and room for commendation—helps them to move along confidently. When they make mistakes—especially with their children—they need the assurance that life's outcome is not determined by one situation and that kids who are loved are resilient.

Constant nagging, disapproval, and interference are negative and counterproductive. But accepting a passive role on the sidelines of being cheerleaders for our kids can prove traumatic for many grandparents, who are accustomed to getting their hands on the problem. We must realize that "not doing" is a form of "doing" and more effective in the final analysis. As a friend of mine used to say, "There are more sugar horses than whip horses."

Neither my parents or Janie's ever took Psychology 101 or attended a class in parenting or the psychology of the adolescent. Yet we have often commented on how well they did in their task of helping us during our early marriage and the years of child-raising.

In retrospect, we did some pretty stupid things, especially in relationship to my over-zealousness in evangelism and my attempt to reach the whole world of lost youth by myself. Some people pray and wait for opportunities. I go out and find them. At the time of the birth of each of our three children I had blocked off several days in order to be with Janie during these important times. But our doctor had warned us that "they will knock when they are ready to come." In all three cases, the babies came either earlier or later than planned, and I was out of the state when they "knocked."

To her everlasting credit, Janie has never held this up to me even in times of stress. My mother was at the hospital with her each time and my dad drove the car. We brought the babies home to Janie's parents' house, and my parents never did add their words of chagrin or chastisement to my sense of disappointment and regret.

My parents had ample opportunities to question our call to Christian youth work, our financial decisions and our parenting skills, but they never did. We were conscious every minute of their example, support, and love.

Recently I was speaking with a young mother at her mother-in-law's funeral. "My mother-in-law always believed in me and gave me confidence in myself," she said. "She always made me feel very special. She rarely gave unsolicited advice, but when she did you could count on her sound judgment."

At the opposite pole, a confused and somewhat angry father shared his feelings of disappointment and resignation. "My mother brings things for the grandkids, but they have strings attached. You have to acknowledge constantly that she gave them to your kids, then when the kids grow up she expects eternal gratitude from them for all she has done. She expects perfection from my kids as she did from me, and as a result they shy away from visiting her."

A teenager told how she felt unloved and rejected by her parents. "I miss my grandparents," she said. "They had the extra time to listen, to go fishing and stuff. They set time aside for me because I suppose they knew I was only going to be around for a few days at a time. And besides, they didn't know all of my faults like my parents do."

Her words reminded me of Jesus with Peter. Jesus obviously knew Peter's faults, but still he called him *Petros,* a Rock, to affirm in him his best side. If we can do that as cheerleader for our own grown children, we will give them an invaluable gift.

HANDS ON

In addition to the passive, "hands-off" role of cheerleader, grandparents can also fulfill an active, "hands-on" role of interpreter. We can interpret the parents to the grandchildren and grandchildren to parents.

Interpreting love. When we spend time with our grandchildren, inevitably they talk about what's going on at home. Sometimes they gripe and complain about discipline and restrictions. We find it very important to listen and to hear them out and then give them another point of view: "It may seem like Mom is hard on you, but did you ever think what it would be like if she didn't care about you? The reason she tells you this is because she loves you and doesn't want you to be hurt." Or we can say, "It may seem like your folks are a little strict, but they're strict because they care. Would you really like to have parents who didn't ask questions, or tell you when to be home, who didn't care what kinds of things you watch on TV, or who didn't care if you lie? Your parents do this because they love you." I find that most kids would rather be over-loved than under-loved.

At a Youth for Christ camp one summer, a boy came up to me, sat down on the other end of a porch bench, and said, "My parents don't love me."

I said, "Come on. Of course, they do."

"Don't give me that!" he said. "I know you're supposed to say that to kids, but it's not true in my case."

"How do you know?" I asked.

"Well," he began, "our neighbors have a little black and white spotted dog. He's not a purebred or anything, but they love him. If he doesn't come in at night, they go up and down the street yelling, 'Here, Spotty! Here, Spotty!' They even make phone calls and disturb the neighbors. They don't go to bed until he's home, safe and sound. Me? I come and go as I please and nobody ever asks a question. Our neighbors love their dog—my parents don't love me!"

Interpreting finances. In a world of TV commercials and materialism, family finances often need interpretation. We can help our grandchildren understand that their folks are not the money tree, and that, "Even though your parents work very hard, nobody has enough money to buy everything you see on TV. The reason they don't have certain things is not because of a lack of love but because there's only so much money to go around. It doesn't hurt to want sometimes." We can tell them about times when we've had less than we have now and how we learned to be happy without all the material things.

They will often find this well-worn speech tedious because it goes crossgrain to their selfishness. But they *will* remember. As we intrepret financial reality to our grandchildren, they gain appreciation of their parents and have a little broader understanding of the place of money in a Christian's life.

Interpreting reality. Another hands-on role grandparents can fill is the role of realist. By interpreting reality to our grandchildren, we help them see that some of their requests and desires are not as reasonable as they think they are. We say "No, not every kid in the world really does have these things. Not everybody gets to do what they want. It's a bigger world than you think it is."

☙

*In family life, as in politics,
united we stand, divided we fall.*

Parents often become weary of trying to explain to children the reasons why they must say "no" to certain requests. A grandparent, in a more relaxed atmosphere, can sometimes help children to see that compared with all the people in the world, they really have a pretty good life. We can constantly interpret reality for them so that they can see their true position. If their lives are indeed difficult, unjust, or impossible, taking sides or driving a wedge between parent and child will not help. In family life, as in politics, united we stand, divided we fall.

Many times children think their parents are just making excuses and are involved in a verbal tug of war for control. Most often, however, parents impose restrictions out of economic necessity or to teach discipline and maturity.

At Taylor University where I work, one-third of all students travel overseas before graduating. They are involved in study opportunities, cultural exchanges and various forms of Christian witness. Though I am confident the purposes for which they travel abroad are effective, the most evident value most share when they return home is the observation that of all the people on the globe, Americans are the most privileged. They suddenly realize that many people spend their entire lives simply surviving, and that things we take for granted are really wonderful bonuses provided at great effort and sacrifice by others.

I often wonder about the two-thirds of the students at Taylor who do not gain this insight from global travel. Who will teach them these lessons? Will they be left to learn their values from the media?

る

When grandparents share the longer and larger view that they have gained from life's experiences, they can reinforce the truths that parents attempt to teach without encountering the same resistance that parents experience. Grandparents, after all, are expected to be a little quaint.

Sometimes young people get caught in a trap of seeing only their own family and a few neighborhood families around them. They need someone who has been around a little while who can see the bigger picture and tell them how the rest of the world really is. When grandparents share the longer and larger view that they have gained from life's experiences, they can reinforce the truths that parents attempt to teach without encountering the same resistance that parents experience.

Grandparents, after all, are expected to be a little quaint. They can get away with saying, "Yes, I know you have this particular problem, but have you thought about your parents' larger situation? Your parents pay for the house, buy the food, and have demands on them daily. They work hard to make a living, and if they spend all their time playing with you, meeting your demands, the family will sink. You must understand that your folks live in a competitive world. Sometimes they have to be gone at night or on the weekend."

As we interpret reality to our grandchildren, we help them understand that their parents are not guilty of some terrible sin by not spending all their time with them. Kids need to know that their parents' lives are not like TV sitcoms and that parents have heavy responsibilities on them.

This can be difficult for children to understand, especially if they are in an affluent church where other parents seem to have all the time in the world and children seem to have all the toys and playthings they could imagine. Grandparents can help their grandchildren see that there will always be people who have more than they do, but that they are very fortunate to have what they have in comparison with the larger world. We must interpret reality for our grandchildren so that they don't spend their time feeling sorry for themselves.

Interpreting life. Many kids, of course, really do not get enough of their parent's attention. Sometimes this is the result of legitimate economic pressures and sometimes it is the result of careerism or lust for things or power. But I'm convinced that kids are both resilient and insightful. If they sense that their folks really want to spend time with them but simply cannot, they are for the most part understanding and supportive, even if they are disappointed. If they feel, however, that they are a fifth wheel and not really very important on their parents' priority list, they will react out of a sense of rejection or heartbreak.

In such cases grandparents can do little to rectify the causes, but we can provide support, assurance, and love to help lessen the tension and give a grandchild enough security to keep him or her from going over the edge. We never know the specific tolerance level of any individual. Some can absorb great deprivation, while others are triggered by seemingly trivial circumstances. A little loving prevention can be the critical ingredient.

A college student confided to me, "My parents had great difficulty dealing with everyday life and had many personal problems brought about by the stress of their jobs and their relationship. My maternal grandparents were both very talented people and had many interests and hobbies. We took trips to the library, boating, swimming and talking. They taught me structure and organization and how to live in that kind of environment."

Oftentimes this role of interpreting life means taking the time to listen thoroughly to what our grandchild is feeling and then put it into perspective. I have watched my mother do this with her grandchildren, and I'm amazed at how many phone calls she receives from grandsons and granddaughters who bounce their ideas off her. They do most of the talking; she says "Uh-huh," and listens to them lay out the situation, then she throws in carefully-worded statements to help them get their bearings. She reminds them that they aren't the only people who have had small children and who have felt restricted and circumscribed by the demands of their family. She reminds them that this, too, will pass and that life will move on to other stages.

My mother's attention gives her grandchildren a feeling that all is well. Somehow or another, in the ebb and flow of life, things will work out and be all right after all. Her grandchildren see her as a "pioneer woman"—and in more ways than one, they are right.

Last summer we were at the lake with my mother and our extended family. One of our grandsons, Benjamin, woke up gasping for air. We rushed him to the local hospital, but by the time we arrived, his symptoms were decidedly better. The attending physician explained that often the cold night air sometimes reverses the effect of an asthma attack, and by the time the frightened parents get to the hospital, everything is all right.

On the way home my mother told the girls her memory of a baby born prematurely, long before doctors really knew how to deal with the situation. They kept the baby on the back porch in the cold, warmly wrapped in blankets, and it had survived and grown into a normal child. She told of children she knew who had outgrown their asthma and were normal adults. The girls stared at each other and then gazed at Grandma in wonder, as if she possessed some primal knowledge not available to their generation.

Mother would laugh at this, of course: she is in no way an advocate of the return to folk medicine. What she has is not magic, but experience.

I was very touched by the story told to me by a young mother who had been deserted by her husband. She was trying to believe in herself and cope with a future that was filled with uncertainties.

"If my grandma could do it," she said, "I can do it. After grandpa died her house was destroyed by fire. Years later it was destroyed by a tornado. She never gives up, yet she is fun to be around. She loves to play cards, especially "sneaky" games like, "nickel knock," "spoons," and "old maid." She prefers reading to TV, loves to travel, and is facing the realities of old age with grace. She gave me my first Bible and taught me Bible verses and how to pray."

This young woman's remembrance, complete in its simplicity, shows how courage and virtue can be a wonderful polestar for a troubled, lonely, frightened young woman determined to make the best of a tough situation. I wonder if her grandma knows—or even suspects—what a profound influence she has had? A wise person once said, "What you are and what you believe are the most important things about you."

❧

The role of grandparenting is the role of a stabilizer on an aircraft. We don't provide the power like the engine. We don't provide direction like the rudder. We're the stabilizer that keeps things steady in the air.

In some ways the role of grandparenting is a shift from an active, doing role to a more passive, observing role. It's the role of a stabilizer on an aircraft. We don't provide the power like the engine. We don't provide direction like the rudder. The parents do these things. We're the stabilizer that keeps things steady in the air. We're there. We provide perspective. We help our grown children stay steady while they do what they must do as parents. We provide the support to keep our grandchildren on board while the parents are doing their best.

It may be fine for a grandmother to have her grandchildren call her Karen, but somehow I think young people have enough Karens around them. What they need is someone with a little more experience, a little more mileage, a few more wrinkles; someone who has failed more often and overcome failure; someone who has been disappointed and found the strength to cope; someone who has seen a storm or two arise and has seen it through to the finish; someone who's endured pain and overcome it, who can bring the longer view of experience to daily life.

Our role as grandparents is not the same as the role of the hands-on parent. We don't get a chance to raise a family the second time. We do get a chance, however, carefully and tactfully to nudge, to love, and to influence. When we take our hands off as controllers, we can put our hands back on as interpreters—of love, of finances, of reality, of life.

FOUR

Putting Down Roots

JANIE AND I are about the age of the grandparents of most of our students. We are often invited to come to residence halls to do question-and-answer sessions on male/female relationships or dating and marriage. The students are very interested in what it was like when we were young.

One of the first questions is usually, "How did you meet and what did you do while you were courting?"

Janie almost always replies, "To begin with, we didn't *court*, we *dated*. Our parents courted." I chuckle at her defensiveness about the use of the word "court," but it does betray a kind of bias young people have about the past and about us as grandparents.

When I have the chance to speak to college students, I try to share some rather transparent situations aimed at helping them to realize that we struggled with many, if not most, of the anxieties and temptations that they face in today's world. I try to be candid about the fact that we had sexual temptations, that we necked in the back seat of automobiles and had to pray for self-control. We try, tastefully, to let them know that we still have a sex life, that growing older does not mean settling for less intimacy or intensity, but that these things grow in the context of Christian marriage. Too often youth seeks to achieve in variety of sexual experience what only intimacy and trust can provide. We try to show them, by example, that maturity does not mean "going to seed."

ﻪﻬ

Maturity does not mean "going to seed."

THE ROOTS OF FAITH

Janie and I accept these invitations hoping to help students realize that the past can inform the present, that they are not on their own trying to work their way through uncharted waters. I am amazed to discover that many young people seem to have no knowledge about their parents' or grandparents' personal lives—the fact that they are real, living human beings with drives, desires, aspirations, fears, frustrations, anxieties, regrets, and hopes. Yet I believe it is is important for mature adults to risk exposure and misunderstanding in an attempt to communicate with youth.

God has chosen to be transparent and self-revelatory in his communication with us. The characters in the Bible are not inventions of a public relations expert. They envy, kill, commit adultery, connive, deceive, love, lust, abandon, exhibit courage and cowardice. In short, they exemplify the whole range of human experience. And the Bible has to be that honest if it is to be credible. A public relations person would have removed the ambiguity and failure in order to make the product more salable. But God gave us a Word that is believable and relevant to a fallen race.

We do not have to read long in the Old Testament to discover the basic theme and story line: God has been faithful to us in the past; we can, therefore, depend on him today and for the future. The future hinges on the faithfulness of God. "He is the same yesterday, today and forever." God will never fail us; our happiness and success in the long run is tied to learning the lessons of history. God helped the people in the Bible through their problems, and he can help us, too.

৯&

The future hinges on the faithfulness of God.

In Joshua chapter four, the children of Israel had just crossed over the Jordan River on dry land. Joshua commanded the leader of each tribe to take one stone out of the river bed and carry it with them. He then told them to make a monument out of the stones. "In the future, when your children ask you, 'What do these stones mean?'" he said, "tell them that the flow of the Jordan was cut off before the ark of the covenant of the Lord. When it crossed the Jordan, the waters of the Jordan were cut off. These stones are to be a memorial to the people of Israel forever" (Jos 4:6-7).

We, too set up memorial stones—systems and traditions that remind us of God's faithfulness. But often our children and grandchildren are never really answered when they ask, "What do these stones mean?"

To large degree, grandparents bear the responsibility of keeping the past alive, reminding others of the faithfulness of God. We can do that, in part, by telling our stories. All ancient people have traditions of storytelling. The stories are preserved from generation to generation, and this combined wisdom provides the foundation on which culture is built.

THE CUT FLOWER GENERATION

Elton Trueblood, a distinguished Quaker theologian, has called this generation "the cut flower generation"— rootless, without a past or a foundation. Their story starts with, "In the beginning God created me." Life has a sense of "nowness" or immediacy to it. Today's big news wraps tomorrow's garbage.

I believe the problems of our culture are largely a result of young people not knowing the lessons of history and thus being destined to repeat the mistakes of the past. And our problems are not merely social issues, but theological ones as well.

Alexander Solzhenitsyn laid all the difficulties of the Soviet Union on the fact that they had forgotten God. The Communist government made it illegal for families to maintain their religious heritage. Only the very committed were able to sustain their faith in the face of persecution. In America we face the challenge of sustaining ours in the face of indifference and self-preoccupation.

We often talk about the spiritual emptiness of the Communist system and the scandal of religious oppression in the Soviet bloc. Yet we who can worship freely and have the opportunity to maintain Christian culture are opting not to do so—either out of a twisted understanding of separation of church and state or out of sheer spiritual indifference on the part of many of our generation. Many older people simply do not want any family responsibility after their own nest is empty.

A faculty member from Lobatchevsky State University (formerly Gorky State University) in Russia spoke to me about her spiritual concerns for her teenage son. "My parents' generation is spiritually lost," she said. "They have no spiritual life to share with anyone. They gave themselves wholeheartedly to the revolution, and now that it has failed and collapsed, they are disillusioned, withdrawn, and alcoholic. This is true of an entire generation. If our children are to have any spiritual example, they must get it from their parents, and this is a difficult task. Grandparents are very important, almost indispensable, to spiritual communication."

CULTURE-CARRIERS

As the Russian professor indicated, grandparents serve the function of being culture-carriers. They glean, out of a lifetime of experience, several important lessons and blessings of their lives, and then pass them on to the current generation.

One class I teach, in Christian youth ministry, has opened my eyes to this generation's lack of understanding about its roots. In the class we discuss youth society, youth culture, and how we arrived at the particular place we are in modern America. Beginning with the students' grandparents' generation, we develop a timeline establishing the various important events of World War II. We discuss the Allies, who our enemies were, the alliance between Germany and Japan, the Holocaust, the atom bomb, the rebuilding of Europe, the emergence of Japan as an economic force, and the place of various characters of the period—Eisenhower, MacArthur, Roosevelt, Truman, Churchill. We try to understand the foundations upon which their grandparents' lives are built.

❧

Grandparents serve the function of being culture-carriers. They glean out of a lifetime of experience, several important lessons and blessings of their lives, and then pass them on to the current generation.

Then we talk about their parents' generation—Vietnam; the drug culture; the Civil Rights movement; Martin Luther King Jr.; Timothy Leary; political figures like John F. Kennedy and Richard Nixon; and significant turning points such as Watergate. I try to help them understand their parents' perspectives against the backdrop of the sixties.

Most of these "familiar" events, however, are totally new to my students. They don't know the recent history of this country. But when I begin to talk to them about their grandparents, when I ask them to tell me their grandfather's 'story,' they immediately know what I mean.

"My grandfather's story is about the Great Depression," one student told me. "His emphasis is on the fact that you have to work hard and save money because some day bad things will happen and bad times will come along. You'll be surprised that things aren't as easy as they are now. You will be caught without anything in the bank, and you'll be destitute if you don't live conservatively."

Another student said that her grandfather's story is about the Second World War. "He says it was a 'real' war, not like those of today, a war when there were definite good guys and bad guys. My grandfather is very patriotic and gets teary-eyed at the American flag and the place of America in the world. He's negative about the Japanese and doesn't think we should purchase Japanese-made products." These students may not know history, but they know their grandparents' stories.

But when I ask them to "tell me your father's story," they become very quiet. Their fathers, it seems, don't *have* a story. Most of their parents were "sixties people" who lived against the backdrop of the sexual revolution, the drug culture, and confusing political times. Many struggled with whether they should serve in the armed forces or go to Canada. Sometimes their parents weren't involved but were just surrounded by the sixties environment and aren't sure about themselves.

These young people will not be getting a story from their parents until their parents become certain about their own. Most are clear in their Christian commitment but unsure about other issues. As they grow older, they will be able to sort out their experiences and feel more solid about what they want to pass on to their children. In the meantime, the task falls to the grandparents to be culture-carriers for their grandchildren.

ESTABLISHING THE PATTERN

Sharing our story—the lessons of life, values, and anchor points that are implanted in our minds—is important for the establishing of our grandchildren's roots.

One of my grandpa's favorite stories was about cutting rafters for a barn. The neighbor's barn had burned down, so the neighbors all got together for a "barn raising." The women baked pies and fried chicken and prepared all sorts of good things to eat. The men went to work on great piles of lumber to build the barn. Apparently a few had some carpentry skills, and those with experience laid out the rafters. They made a pattern and set the younger men to cutting the rafters.

By noon they had a few rafters in place, and while the men were sitting around eating pie and looking at the building, they noticed the barn looked a little crooked. Something was wrong. Soon they realized that the young men had taken the pattern, cut one rafter, marked the second, and laid it aside. They marked the third from the second, the fourth from the third, and so on. Each time they cut a rafter, they used the previous rafter as a pattern.

And each time, they gained the length of one pencil mark. By the time a hundred rafters were cut, there was a discrepancy of more than a foot.

Grandpa would tell this story and slap his knee and tell how funny this was and the valuable lesson learned. He was attempting to pass on his experience about the problem of gradualism: each time we make a little change or compromise our morals, we move further from the truth. We get further and further from the standard, until at last we find ourselves in real trouble.

ぇ&

As grandparents who love and follow Christ, we can give them a pattern of right- eousness that will help them build a life strong enough to withstand the elements.

Grandpa's rafter story has another application. In mod- ern life, young people desperately need reliable patterns from which to cut the supporting rafters of their lives. As grandparents who love and follow Christ, we can give them a pattern of righteousness that will help them build a life strong enough to withstand the elements.

WHAT DO THESE STONES MEAN?

Because our children and grandchildren need those patterns, the Scriptures tell us not to forsake the assembling of ourselves together. As we gather each week around the Word of God, we affirm the importance of the Scripture in our lives. We establish a pattern of reverence for God and his Word.

Grandparenting gives us the opportunity to pass on the long view, the big picture about life with Christ. We have overcome obstacles, learned lessons, and matured in our faith. God has been faithful to us, and now as we apply these truths in the present, we can still depend on him to be with us. And when young people ask us why we do these things—or in Old Testament language, "What do these stones mean?"—we have the chance to tell them about the faithfulness of God.

Some of my own students, in relating their grandparents' stories, discover "what these stones mean"—that is, how the "old ways," the principles by which their grandparents lived, apply to their own lives.

1. True happiness is not found in material accumulations. "Sometimes I think I would be much happier if I had a really neat car, better clothes, an awesome stereo," one student said. "But my granddad always reminds me that true happiness is not found in material accumulations. He and Grandma didn't have a lot in those days, and yet I think they were happier than I am because they really loved each other. So maybe 'keeping up with the Joneses' really is a waste of time. If there's love in the family, like my granddad and grandma have, being rich or poor is less important."

I could listen to a thousand sermons on the subject of materialism and not hear truth spoken with as much power as in this one testimonial. These students really believe what their grandparents say; they have fire in their eyes and passion in their hearts. And if these passionate young people decide to be school teachers, missionaries, or social workers instead of setting their sights on higher paying professions, they will give a great deal back to our society. From their grandparents they have learned that value is not related to material reward, and success is not measured by the size of a paycheck.

2. It's never right to do wrong to get a chance to do right. "Whenever I am tempted to cut corners, cheat, or rationalize my way through something," another student confessed, "I hear my grandmother's voice and think again. I admire my grandmother and trust her. I want her to be proud of me."

Vince Lombardi, coach of the once invincible Green Bay Packers, was often asked the secret of his coaching success. He always replied, "fundamentals." Football is about blocking, tackling, running, and catching the ball. Successful players, however, tended to think that they were so good they could violate the basics and succeed. Lombardi took college All-Americans and insisted they return to the fundamentals of basic football. And he won more football games than any coach in his time.

3. We reap what we sow; the chickens always come home to roost. "My grandparents meant that we'd better put in the effort if we expect things to turn out right someday," a student told me. "A lot of my high school friends party all the time and spend all their money on drugs and cars. When I get discouraged about college, when things are rough, I'm tempted to chuck it all and live like my friends. But then I remember what my grandparents said, and I know they're right."

4. A person's word is his bond. "My grandfather taught me that you ought to be able to trust somebody without a contract or putting it in writing," one young woman said. "I like that, and I try to be a person who can be trusted."

5. If a man's wife can't trust him, you can't trust him either. "My grandparents have a great marriage," another student said. "He treats my grandma like a queen. A lot of men I know have cheated on their wives or ignored them, but not my grandpa. He's trustworthy." Grandchildren may sometimes look through rose-colored glasses, but many understand the underlying truth expressed.

These young people are profoundly impressed by folk wisdom when it comes from their grandparents. The principles they express may seem like pat answers, but the seed of truth is there—a seed that is watered and cultivated into a strong, healthy root system by grandparents who live what they preach. As Robert McNamara used to quip on television panel shows, "The trouble with clichés is that they are almost always true."

THE ROOTS GROW DEEP
WHEN THE WINDS ARE STRONG

Once, during an Insight for Living conference, I heard Chuck Swindoll quote his mother as saying, "The roots grow deep when the winds are strong." I never knew his mother, but I do know something about West Texas and what it meant to raise a family during the depression in that part of America. I noted the look in the eyes of the adult Swindoll kids and could sense the impact. Their grandmother taught them about perseverance, about overcoming adversity, about holding on when you want to give up. Her faith stood as an example that God is faithful, and that God works in every situation for the good of those who love him.

This is a convincing kind of heritage to pass on. Young people on the edge of suicide might hang on and persevere if they had a statement like that in their memory.

Our children have an excellent example in Janie's parents. Janie's older sister Elaine was born with a birth defect, and for all practical purposes was paralyzed from the neck down. By the time our kids were born, she was in her late thirties. Elaine was very bright, both intellectually and temperamentally, yet she was restricted to sitting Buddha-like in her bed or in a wheelchair for short periods.

Our children watched their grandparents care for Aunt Elaine all the years that they were growing up. They were largely unaware of the sacrifice and dedication that their grandparents exhibited, because that's the way it was always done. They saw in Janie's mother a devotion that never faded. She literally spent every day—with the exception of one week of vacation (in fifty years)—in the same room with Elaine, caring for her every need. She did all of this without complaint or hints for sympathy. Every Sunday Grandpa Smith patiently lifted Elaine into her wheelchair, pushed her up the ramp into his van, and took her to church, never without a smile.

Now that the grandparents are dead, the kids realize that they have witnessed truly heroic behavior. All of us who knew their situation intimately, marvel at the quality of life of two ordinary people who simply lived out their lives in faith and obedience to Jesus Christ in the midst of great sacrifice. As someone once said, "I slept and dreamed that life was joy. I awoke and found that life was duty. I did my duty and God gave me joy!" They lived out their story quietly and without fanfare, and it is written indelibly on all of us.

Grandparents have the opportunity and responsibility to remind young people that God will never leave them nor forsake them, that he has been faithful to us in the past and therefore He will be faithful in the present. We can share stories of answered prayer, of times when God came to our rescue, when He did things for us that we didn't understand.

Janie and I have told our children the story of our own experience with tithing, how God has never disappointed us. We have not only attempted to tithe, but to go above the tithe in our giving to Christ and his church and to the needy and poor. We've tried to explain to them that mathematically it doesn't work. In math, nine-tenths shouldn't go as far as ten-tenths; but in life's experience, if you lay aside the first portion and give it to the Lord and his work, God will bless you, "shaken together, pressed down, and running over," as the Scripture says.

We have been gratified to see our children practicing the same principle and passing it on to our grandchildren. These testimonies to God's faithfulness, of seeing us through, have value. Our children and grandchildren live in a demanding and competitive culture, where expenses rise to meet income and every dollar has a couple of places to be used. It is easy to rationalize that charitable needs are covered by our taxes, that somebody else can take care of them, that there are a lot of people richer than we are who should carry the responsibility. But our example of tithing has made an impact on our lives, and we want to pass it on to our children and our children's children.

A grandmother told me that she and her husband sat down with a tape recorder and made a cassette for each of their grandchildren in which they shared their personal testimony as well as a kind of spiritual oral history of their lives together. They shared the lessons that they learned, a little bit about their memories of what their children were like when they were children and teenagers, and their hopes and dreams for each of them. Fifty years from now their grandchildren's grandchildren can hear the voices of these grandparents and have a handle on the heritage of their faith.

❧

*Our experiences will give them "stones"
in their lives which, combined with their
own experience of God's goodness,
will enable them to build an altar of
remembrance unto the Lord.*

In Sunday school, children are taught to sing "Count your blessings, name them one by one...." It might be of great value to us as grandparents to take time to start at the beginning of our experience—perhaps the beginning of our marriage together—and list the examples of God's faithfulness in our lives during this period. Then, during times of family conversation, we can share with our grandchildren these signs of God's faithfulness and his provision. Our experiences will give them "stones" in their lives which, combined with their own experience of God's goodness, will enable them to build an altar of remembrance unto the Lord.

FIVE

Finding the Common Ground

T HE AIRPLANE'S ENGINE was on fire!

I awoke from a brief nap and looked out the window to my right to see the engine below the wing blazing. I had flown hundreds of thousands of miles and had never seen anything like this happen before.

Around me, others had noticed, but most sat in a stunned silence, not knowing what to do or say about it. As the various passengers became aware of what was going on, the pilot's voice came over the intercom: "You may have noticed that the right wing of our aircraft is on fire. We have fire extinguishers built into the plane and are trying to extinguish it. In fact, I think we've succeeded. What you are now seeing is smoke, but we believe the fire is out." He explained that the plane had safety devices that shut off the fuel to the engine and pumped the fuel from that particular wing into another tank.

The black smoke began to subside a bit, but there

remained some white, fog-like smoke that trailed along behind the wing. The pilot indicated that this particular plane—and, indeed, most airplanes—have a redundancy built into them that allows them to fly with one engine. He said we would attempt to go down to a lower altitude and try to land at a military base where they had equipment to help.

We began our descent and flew down toward Lake Superior, close enough to see the whitecaps on top of the waves. I remembered reading about the temperature of Lake Superior and how long one could survive in it, and I began to write a note to my wife, Janie. I was not totally convinced that we would die, but on the other hand I thought that—just in case—I would leave her a message. I wrote a long note and placed it inside my Bible, remembering that books, at least the inside pages, tended to survive through floods and fires.

To my amazement, once the pilot had given these words of assurance and we began to fly along fine, people settled down to the routine of a typical commercial flight. We were trusting the experts. We eventually landed on a foam-covered runway lined on both sides with the blinking red lights of fire engines. But the thought crossed my mind that we were getting used to something we've no business getting used to.

My misgivings were confirmed when we landed and I had a short discussion with the flight crew. They indicated how tense it was in the cockpit, that they had no idea whether we really could land safely. They had actually feared for their lives.

It may be possible to limp along on one engine, but it is definitely better to fly the plane the way it was designed to fly.

FLYING ON A BROKEN WING

As I thought about my experience, and how people seemed to accept it as "normal," I realized that abnormal things are happening all around us and are matter-of-factly reported to us by the media. We have become so accustomed to them that we have begun treating them as if they are normal circumstances. I believe we have raised an entire generation who have seen addiction, violence, and sexual promiscuity so often that they perceive those activities as normal. Some have become used to them because they have never known anything else, others have learned to earn their livings by "putting out fires" and have opted for a life of social salvage. Those who live in the cockpit, those who are in the helping professions—such as counselors, psychologists, social workers, pastors, teachers, and lawyers—are daily in contact with the cultural dysfunctions and still see them as dysfunctions. Though their livelihood depends on these dysfunctions existing in culture, they would gladly change their means of earning a living to see these things changed.

❧

We have raised an entire generation who have seen addiction, violence, and sexual promiscuity so often that they perceive these activities as normal.

It amazes me what lengths people go to in order to try to live with dysfunction. Recently I saw a television program about deaf children. A doctor had developed a device which, when implanted behind the ear of a deaf child, could provide an experience very close to hearing. One particular child was featured and filmed as she experienced the world of hearing for the first time. Her ecstasy was evident as her face beamed upon hearing sounds of mother and music. I thought, *Isn't this terrific? I hope it works for all deaf people!*

To my amazement the reporters on the program began to interview various people in the deaf world—people who ran schools for the deaf, people who had gone through training in order to be able to sign and to communicate. These were noble people who had in many cases learned to cope in this culture with distinction. They were opposed to this medical procedure because deafness was not an abnormality or some sort of dysfunction, but was just another form of normalcy. Based on their experience, people were better off deaf because of the many ways they learned to cope; their compensatory behavior was superior to hearing.

I could hardly believe that anyone would think that a person bereft of one of the major senses would be better off without it. I understood that people have, indeed, achieved much even though they were deaf. But taking the argument a step further to say that the dysfunction is actually an "alternative reality" and that we shouldn't try to help people out of it is incomprehensible.

Among many parents and young people today there is a great deal of anger at the very idea of a traditional family. Many of these people have known great disappointment and pain in their own lives, because they have been raised in families of dysfunction, and they have struggled nobly to overcome adversity. Thus, understandably, they try to justify to their friends the fact that they are just as good as anyone else, even though their families were torn apart by divorce or alcohol or abandonment. No fair person would deny them this distinction. Most of them deserve our admiration. Many, however, in an attempt to compensate, are actually angry at the very concept of normalcy.

THE DEATH OF THE BRADY BUNCH

Half a generation ago, American family life was represented by television shows like "The Brady Bunch." Some critics say that the program represented domestic commitment and tranquility that never existed in the first place, or at least not in their personal experience. Others, having taken a course or two in urban sociology, feel it is unfair to present such a responsible and happy family to people who have no hope of attaining such a life. Most seem to feel that family life has moved so far away from this adjusted, devoted nuclear family that it is silly to perpetrate the idea itself.

When we watch a few reruns of this familiar icon of a former America and compare it with any of several "family-oriented" sit-coms currently running, certain questions arise: "What is so wrong with the Brady Bunch?" or "What makes Dr. Huxtable (the character developed by Bill Cosby) such a lightning rod for criticism?"

To be sure, the families are intact and they live in middle class surroundings, but don't a lot of people? Why not be critical instead of the salaries of the media and academic people making the observations—or, for that matter, rock stars with their false identification with the poor, or athletes who have escaped poverty through athletic endowments and never look back at those who they have left behind?

There seems to be another reason that these simple half-hour family morality plays have been the target of so much criticism. They seem to be the last symbol of a lost dream, even perhaps a primal longing for stability, love, and values in a self-oriented culture that is not really as happy with itself as it wants to be. Society is not quite ready for repentance and honest evaluation of where its values have led. Society wants a way out—provided, of course, that the way out does not involve obedience and scriptural values and an abandonment of personal hedonism.

We are aware of the deep pain, the conflict of modern life, and the terrible situations in which people find themselves. Yet we still hark back to functional families and traditional families and say that it is better to have one's senses restored than to learn nobly to accept the handicap. No amount of changing vocabulary can change the very real pain that people experience. Grandparents cannot, like the Lone Ranger, "return to those thrilling days of yesteryear," but they can patiently, prayerfully and insightfully attempt to understand what is going on in this society, and begin to develop individual strategies to buttress the collapsing family structure. And to do that we need to understand the culture which is shaping our grandchildren.

֍

No amount of changing vocabulary
can change the very real pain that
people experience.

THE FRAGMENTED FAMILY

In contemporary society, one of the most obvious factors which makes this generation different from our generation is the divorce rate. The divorce rate in America has increased 700 percent in this century. There is one divorce today for every 1.8 marriages, and as a result thirteen million children have one or both parents missing.

Even the most liberal of sociologists usually agree that it is better for a child to have two parents rather than one, that a child needs to live in security rather than in an atmosphere of fear and anxiety. It is no easy task for a young person to adjust to a blended family or a new stepparent. Thus, we must conclude that the divorce rate and the ease with which people break up marriages is a serious issue.

All airline personnel as well as those of us who fly a great deal share the common experience of watching children of divorce being loaded onto flights by gate attendants to fly unaccompanied across the continent. I've sat next to many such children over the years and am always shaken up a bit by this experience. Frankly, I've felt that the children often handle it better than I do. They seem like boarding school children worldwide: *stiff upper lip, don't cry, you're a big boy now.*

As I sit next to them and watch them begin the trip, organizing their new travel toys on the tray table and busying themselves with airline food, I sense that I have met a new kind of child—a truly self-sufficient modern. As the trip progresses, however, certain unmistakable characteristics of children everywhere begin to break through—the nervous chatter that all of us resort to in times of insecurity; attempts to write to Mama, even though the flight is barely two hours old; the clutching of the stuffed animal and the question, "Mister, would you mind if I go to sleep on your shoulder?"

I am not able to make the judgment that all divorce is wrong. After dealing with hundreds of families, I cannot bring myself to the conclusion that every marriage was made in heaven or that all of them can be salvaged. And I would be the last person to say to a battered woman that she should continue to live with some brutish man either to gain sainthood or to maintain marriage statistics.

But sometimes divorce *can* be avoided and relationships reconciled, if the couple is willing to change. And whenever divorce takes place in a family for whatever reason, there is pain and hurt—not only in the lives of the two people divorcing, but in the lives of parents, children, and friends as well. Society also pays a price in the need for response from the mental health, welfare, school and juvenile justice systems.

We often feel isolated and victimized when divorce hits our families. Yet so many people are affected that even advertising has found the subject profitable. In a recent television commercial, two well-dressed women stand together under an umbrella in front of an upscale restaurant. One of the women seems distraught as she tells the other of her impending divorce. Her friend has a look of knowing compassion, as if all women will eventually have to face the same situation. As viewers we wonder, *Where is the hook? I know they are selling something; I wonder what it is?* We are then told that Paine Webber understands and can help a woman in this situation plan for her future, independent of any man.

In daily contact with college students, I find that, almost universally, young women plan for living alone and taking care of themselves. This once was a response to the longer life of women and the prospect of widowhood. But today many young women are choosing not to marry at all. And for those who *do* plan to marry, their experience with abandonment and divorce has made them wary of marital commitment; they hedge their bets. Furthermore, the expectation that marriages will break up lends a kind of social sanction to divorce.

If we, as grandparents who love God and believe in the family, intend to help shore up the weak places, we must understand the pervasive and central place of divorce in our grandchildren's lives, and its ripple effect on their personal, psychological, and spiritual well-being.

ঽৡ

Putting human beings in the center has led us to a place where self-interest, personal happiness and pleasure rather than a concern for others or the will of God guides the decision-making process in modern life.

Many are familiar with the writings of the late Francis Schaeffer. One of his concerns was the shift in modern thinking from a universe in which God was the center to one in which man is paramount. Modern society proves that putting human beings in the center has led us to a place where self-interest, personal happiness and pleasure rather than a concern for others or the will of God guides the decision-making process in modern life.

SEX AT THE END OF THE TWENTIETH CENTURY

The so-called "sexual revolution" is another given in the life of today's youth. It would be a mistake to automatically attribute a casual attitude toward sex to our grandchildren individually, but they all live against the backdrop of today's sex-conscious society.

Six hundred thousand unmarried high school pregnancies are carried to term each year in America—about twelve per high school. Many of these young people sit in algebra class with our grandchildren; some of them *are* our grandchildren. These influences are bound to change the way young people look at things. So pervasive is the media influence today that the average young person watches over twenty hours of television per week. If they live to be eighty, our teens will have spent over ten years of their lives in front of the TV set. By age fifteen they have seen up to fifteen thousand acts of violence.

A certain mental impression results from this kind of exposure. Young people have always needed heroes and have always looked up to those in society who embody success or attributes they want to imitate. Abraham Lincoln was that kind of hero to most young people a generation or two ago. And I remember seeing a movie about "Crazylegs Hurst," the football player who overcame physical difficulties and still played football.

Today, however, there seems to be a feeling that elevated ideals must be based on some kind of dishonesty. We therefore emphasize the humanity, even the faults, of our heroes, lest someone escape beyond mediocrity. As a result, our grandchildren have no true heroes to emulate.

Today, young people see professional athletes who are paid more each year than most of their school teachers and principals will make in a lifetime. These "heroes" brag of their sexual conquests—in some cases, numbering in the thousands. It's no wonder young people feel as if their parents are making a federal case out of a minor issue when they have merely become pregnant. Why make such a big deal out of something that can be solved so quickly? Twenty minutes in a doctor's office will take care of the problem, so what's the fuss about?

A recent study by Harvard and MIT entitled, "The Nation's Families 1960-1990," points out that major changes have taken place in the way Americans live together. In 1955, 60 percent of the households in the United States consisted of a working father, a housewife/mother and two or more school age children. In 1980 that previously "typical" family could be found in only 11 percent of American homes, and in 1985 in only 7 percent. It's an astonishing shift in a short period of time—things have changed, radically.

In a recent survey conducted by *Parents* magazine, 77 percent of all adults polled favor sex education in public schools, and two-thirds say that contraceptives should be available in schools with parental consent. Only 29 percent of those polled thought sex education programs should teach children that sex should be saved for marriage; 66 percent said it should be an individual choice. Most published statistics tend toward the conclusion that 80 percent of women and about 95 percent of men have had premarital sex.

No doubt such statistics vary greatly depending on the location and size of the sample, but even if they are 50 percent wrong, they are still alarming. I do not have the advantage of a survey of my own high school, but I know that we lagged considerably behind this survey. Most people my age—both Christian and non-Christian—agree that for our generation, the percentage of sexually active *males* involved in premarital sex was no more than 20 percent. This difference is not simply the result of better statistics gathering. Shifts *are* taking place that affect the way young people think and behave today.

Our grandchildren today are bombarded by society's standards of "acceptable" sexual behavior. They are much more conscious—and conscious much earlier—of their own sexuality and of society's focus on sex. They are faced with school sex education that often teaches them ideas about sexuality that are in opposition to Christian principles of purity. They see sex on television, selling perfume and blue jeans and automobiles; they hear sex in the music that blares from every boom box on the street; they are confronted at every turn by a standard of behavior that encourages exploration and freedom, promiscuity and exploitation. "It's OK to do it," they're told, "as long as you do it with protection."

ह

We can't change society. But what we can do, as grandparents, is to provide for them a solid moral framework, based on biblical principles, to help them establish their own moral standards.

We can't change society—at least not quickly, or all at once. We can't control what our young people see and hear and experience when they are away from us.

But what we *can* do, as grandparents, is to provide for them a solid moral framework, based on biblical principles, to help them establish their own moral standards. We can seek to understand the world they live in, to empathize with their struggles. We can listen. We can love. We can offer guidelines. We can pull them back from the edge.

UNDERSTANDING "THAT AWFUL MUSIC"

I've often said that the thing that makes the "good 'ol days" *good* is poor memory. We can oversentimentalize the past and erase all the heartache and failure, acting as if everything was perfect in earlier generations. But any of us who have lived through it know this is not true. Certain aspects of today's culture are certainly an improvement over the thirties and forties, especially in the areas of technology, communications, transportation, creature comforts, labor saving devices, and medicine. We eat better food than we've ever eaten and spend less of our income on it. Our homes are warmer in the winter and cooler in the summer. Our expectation levels have risen until most young people are able to begin life where their parents left off.

Some of the changes are positive. And as grandparents, we want to learn from this current crop of grandchildren. It's even possible—although unthinkable to many people—that some of their music is superior to some of the pop music that we sang and listened to in our generation. Let's face it—"Mares eat oats and does eat oats and little lambs eat ivy," does lack profundity.

Charlie and Martha Shedd have told an interesting story, related by a grandma who described herself as "somewhat old, somewhat little, and somewhat fat." She said:

I just plain hated rock music! Loud, awful, terrible lyrics. I kid you not, I just plain hated it! Then one day I realized my three teenage grandchildren were drawing away from me. What could I do? One thing I could do was change my tune. I could take another look at their music. So I did. I went to the library and checked out some books on rock music. Then I went to the music store, got into one of those little cubicles they have there, and I really listened to some of this stuff. You may not believe it, but I began to get interested. I even bought some books on the history of rock music and now I have learned some things my grandchildren didn't know. I also kept a little notebook on what I was learning and then I let certain items drop to get their attention.

Next thing I knew they were bringing their friends over to talk rock with Grandma. We'd sit in the den, eat popcorn, and I'd tell them things I'd learned that they didn't know. Then came the great day. The junior high principal called and asked me to speak to 500 kids at his school about rock music. Five hundred kids listening to this fat grandma talk about their music. How'd it go over? If I do say so myself, it went over like gangbusters! And now, hang on. Very shortly after the high school principal called and asked if I'd talk to the high school students. Can you imagine me, the grandma who once hated rock music, there in this huge high school auditorium, and these kids giving me a standing ovation? And what kind of a climate do you think all these shenanigans created between me and my own grandchildren?

Not all of us have the interest or energy for that kind of effort, but we can try to understand our grandchildren's world. Finding the common ground with this generation is rather like what missionaries do in order to win a hearing for the gospel in foreign cultures. We can learn about their world and learn to respect it.

THE MORE THINGS CHANGE,
THE MORE THEY STAY THE SAME

Grandparents often ask me if there is anything that has *not* changed. Actually, quite a bit has remained the same. No matter how radically the *outside* world changes, people are still the same on the *inside*. Growing up, even in an ideal environment, is a traumatic, frustrating, difficult experience. But we as grandparents can help our grandchildren grow up with a minimum of trauma if we remember the common ground we share as human beings.

1. Growing pains. The wonder and confusion of a growing body is the same for our grandchildren as it was for us. Boys are still concerned about whether they will ever be strong enough or tall enough. They worry about their complexions and their emerging sexual awareness. Girls worry about developing a mature figure, wonder if they are attractive to boys, and find the boys in their own class immature and silly. Both boys and girls are extremely insecure about their physical bodies and never find jokes or kidding about these things funny.

Most high schools reward specific physical characteristics that are beyond the control of the kids. If a boy did not have the foresight to have a grandpa over six feet tall, he will probably not play basketball; if a girl has a genetic tendency toward being overweight, she will probably never be a cheerleader. Because so much of their identity is determined by these external issues, our grandchildren have high anxiety about their physical bodies. Protruding ears, crooked teeth and large noses seem like curses from God.

Perhaps this universal childhood anxiety prompted the stories of the "Ugly Duckling" and "The Princess and the

Frog." But whatever the source of the story, the principle is a sound one. Frog kissing is one of the grandparent's strongest weapons against anxiety. We can assure them that time will change many things; we can share stories about our classmates at the twentieth reunion of our high school class. Even if they know these things and have been told them by their teachers and parents, grandparents can reinforce hope for the future by sharing their stories of the past.

ॐ

Grandparents can reinforce hope for the future by sharing their stories of the past.

2. Finding self-acceptance. I recently met a young woman who was deaf at birth. She looks back at her childhood and claims three things that saw her through the pain of being deaf, unable to speak well, and feeling alone and isolated. She was introduced to Jesus Christ at five years of age and was convinced by her parents that Jesus would always be her friend, would be there, and never leave her or forsake her. That gave her a sense of *security*. She remembers holding her head next to her mother's neck and feeling the vibration of her vocal chords while her mother sang to her. That gave her a *song in her heart*. She was encouraged to learn to roller skate and become good at it so much so that she won a trophy. That gave her a sense of competence. Now, in middle age, she is one of the most delightful people I have ever met. *Faith, joy* and *self-worth* are such simple things but they can be everything to a needy child.

When my grandson Wesley and I go fishing, he enjoys being trusted in front of other kids and being independent. I often say, "Why don't you get the boat ready, get the rods, boat cushions, life preservers, and tackle and put it all in the boat. See if there is enough gas and let me know when you are ready." He loves knowing he is completely trustworthy in these tasks. Most of all, he enjoys being trusted in front of others. If there is need for correction, I always try to do it in private and in a soft voice after pointing out all that he did correctly. A teenager told me once, "I can work all day, mow the whole lawn and if I miss one blade of grass, that's what my dad will talk about!" I want Wesley remembering our years together not as a time of frustration, but of affirmation.

3. Finding peer acceptance. Grandparents have a wonderful opportunity to watch their grandchildren grow, to remember how important the small things were and provide affirmation, encouragement, and support when doubt and rejection inevitably creep in. In our youth we all struggled with acceptance in our peer group. Nothing has changed. All of us need friends and will do almost anything to have one. Children are usually proud of their grandparents and want to show us off. A willingness to accept their friends and show interest in them is important in making grandchildren want to be around us. Sometimes kids will show up with strange clothes, haircuts, and earrings. We don't need to panic; these are simply the fads of their generation. I can remember my dad's consternation with my dirty white 'bucks,' black shirt, pink knit tie, and 'D.A.' haircut. Today's Nike shoes with laces dangling and backward baseball caps are no more serious as symbols of degeneration. "This too will pass."

A wise grandparent is able to separate the trivial from the serious. Sometimes it is left to grandparents not to "make mountains out of molehills," "win the battle and lose the war," or "burn down the barn to kill the mice." In a kid's words, "I like my grandparents because they don't always sweat the little stuff."

Adolescents have always worried a lot about friendships and acceptance. Sometimes a grandparent's house is a good place to mope and feel sorry for yourself. It is also a place to get out of the competition of school life and enjoy just being a kid without anyone asking questions about how it's going.

A psychiatrist friend of mine had an old German shepherd that was blind and deaf and barely moved except for the necessities. I mentioned that it looked like it was about time for him to cash in. He said with a laugh, "I hope not. Our grandchildren talk to him, pet him and share all of their problems with him. Actually he does much of what I do day in and day out, except he doesn't charge a fee. So much of mental health is feeling like you are being heard and understood." Sometimes I feel out of touch and a bit baffled by the problems I hear, but I guess all of us can offer the same professional competence as old "Spike."

4. Becoming independent. The struggle between dependence on parents and finding personal identity is one of the most important tasks of growing up. We felt these tensions in our youth and should be able to identify with this struggle. Twenty years ago a popular television commercial bore the tag line, "Mother, please! I'd rather do it myself!" And Jesus delivered a major sermon on this idea. The story of the Prodigal Son relates the experience of a young man who wanted to test his wings. It is also about a father who didn't say, "I told you so." Often young people are not truly in rebellion; they are simply curious about other people, other ways of believing, behaving, and living.

In some cases, the search for independence can take our grandchildren into dangerous waters. Our grandchildren listen to late night talk show hosts and comedians making sophisticated jokes about drug use and give drugs such an aura of respectability that kids feel like country bumpkins unless they have tried them. The road into drugs is a lot easier than the road out and has more cheerleaders. And there is no one quite as lonely as a grandchild trying to kick the drug habit. For thousands, the only friend they have at these times are supportive grandparents—ask any juvenile judge.

But not all of their search for independence is negative. Sometimes they simply want to prove to themselves that they can make it on their own. Many parents have an inordinate need for their kids to be dependent on them because this dependence gives meaning to the parents' lives. Often grandparents are able to see through this confusing condition and provide the assurances that allow young people to develop autonomy and personal accomplishment.

A good deal of youthful frustration is based on this curious tension between dependence and independence. The truth is that children need both—more independence at one time, and less at another. Parenting is an art, not a science, and often grandparents are able to help both children and grandchildren see the source of their conflict. To be able to share their frustration about their parents' smothering love and occasional ineptitude with a grandparent who seems to understand is in itself a release and often an effective therapy.

5. Finding faith. Grandparents are also superbly equipped to deal with another universal, ageless teenage struggle, that of developing one's own faith and value structure. For grandparents raised in somewhat rigid religious backgrounds, this is a familiar struggle. Young people often battle not so much with God as with ideas about God or even faulty and inadequate approaches to God. Sometimes, after being raised in a Christian home, young people simply want to find out how the other half lives. While they are doing this, parents have all kinds of apprehensions.

꒰꒱

Grandparents are superbly equipped to deal with another universal, ageless teenage struggle, that of developing one's own faith and value structure.

I remember the sense of personal affront and deep anxiety I felt when my son decided to attend another church near our home and stopped attending our family church. My feelings were deeply personal; I thought he was rejecting our family and our judgment. I was also fearful because I felt that the church he chose was shallow and might lead him to disillusionment with the entire Christian faith.

Most grandparents have lived long enough to have seen people go through various stages of Christian growth and can handle the diversity while remaining friends with grandchildren and seeing them through these impulses, fads, and flirtations. Many young people go through deep intellectual struggles and find themselves on the backside of the desert, as it were, while sorting through the ambiguities of faith.

Almost all grandparents have either struggled with similar problems at some time in their life or have been associated with someone who has. We are able to be less uptight and threatened than parents and can assume the patient role of the "waiting father" better than parents. One student told me, "Although my parents were totally confused and felt that I was a goner, my grandfather stuck with me as if he had seen it all before. I think it was his faith in me that got me out of the hole I was in. He never gave up on me."

Another student shared about her grandmother: "I could tell her secrets, and she kept them. My folks would have died if they had known what I was going through, but my grandmother kept it to herself. I think that what really helped me was that I knew if my grandma really thought this was totally important and would destroy me or something, she would have spoken. As it was, she listened, understood, and seemed to be saying, 'This will turn out okay, you'll see.' And it did."

❧

We cannot spare them most of the struggles and failures of life. We can, however, demonstrate that after a long life filled with battles and victories, we can come out on the other side and do so with grace.

No area of our lives carries more weight with grandchildren than our faith. As they begin as "babes in Christ" or start their lifelong spiritual pilgrimage, they are, even without knowing it, looking for spiritual maturity. They long to see consistency of life, habits of devotion, fruit of the Spirit, overcoming grace, and above all, the hope of eternal life. We cannot spare them most of the struggles and failures of life. We can, however, demonstrate that after a long life filled with battles and victories, we can come out on the other side and do so with grace.

A young woman who had just become a new Christian wrote, "Because my grandmother lives out of state I could never stay with her, but last summer I went to California at her expense. We played games and went many places. She lives in San Francisco in a small apartment. Life there is much different than life where I live, but mostly it was different because she is a person who prays. Neither of my parents do. Of all the things about her that I love, and the most wonderful gift of all was that she showed me how to have faith in God."

Seemingly small investments can bring enormous returns in the formative lives of young people. We cannot be everything to them, nor can we spare them all of life's difficulties. But what we want to do as grandparents—if we are able—is to teach our grandchildren not to touch every stove to find out if it's hot. We can share with them from our experiences and predict that certain behaviors will bring heartache. When heartache does take place and families are torn apart, we want to be there as grandparents to make all the difference we can make. Sometimes just being there to provide support is the best contribution we can make.

We also need to have the maturity to avoid saying, "I told you so." Taking sides and placing blame accomplishes little. We need to keep our eyes on the target, to bring as much normalcy as possible into difficult situations. There is a tendency on the part of many older people to give up on themselves and feel that they are antiquated and outdated, that the values that have provided the anchor points and compass for their lives no longer work in a modern world.

I joke with parents about this all the time when they tell me about their kids at school learning the new math. "They're teaching different math than when I went to school, and I can't help with homework." I encourage them to get out the math book and start reading at page one. They'll find that 2+2 is still 4, that 8-1 is still 7, and that mathematics has not changed since the beginning of time. Cavemen lining up ten rocks in a row still had to add two more rocks when a couple came to visit. Our hair cuts may not make us look like players in the NBA, and our tennis rackets may have been smaller and made of wood, but math and being an adolescent haven't changed all that much.

૨ะ

When it comes to the basic issues of right and wrong, good and bad, respect and disrespect, instant gratification and making do, cause and effect, reaping what you sow, the costliness of shortcuts, and the heartache connected with breaking God's moral law, there have been no new rules invented.

There is a myth afoot that says that moderns know things that people didn't know before. Yes, they can probably program their calendar watches quicker than we can and do things with a VCR that we haven't yet attempted. But when it comes to the basic issues of right and wrong, good and bad, respect and disrespect, instant gratification and making do, cause and effect, reaping what you sow, the costliness of shortcuts, and the heartache connected with breaking God's moral law, there have been no new rules invented. The grandparent's experience is still valid and needs to be shared. As we open our hearts, our minds and our homes, we find that grandchildren move toward us and welcome our participation and involvement in their lives. After all, we do live at the same moment in history in the same world—and it's our world as well as theirs. We've just been here longer. We've seen a little more and made our own mistakes, and we can share a perspective from a little higher vantage point—even if it is through tri-focals!

SIX

Generations of the Faithful

FIRST JOHN 2:12-14 contains a passage in which John addresses the generations. He writes to children, to young men, and to fathers, and he reveals their various characteristics: "I write to you, dear children, because your sins have been forgiven.... I write to you, fathers, because you have known him who is from the beginning.... I write to you, young men, because you have overcome the evil one."

Interestingly enough, the passage contains the essential characteristics of each generation. This scriptural passage is gender neutral—it speaks of both men and women, the people of God's concern. In reference to biblical culture, this passage speaks of children, parents, and grandparents. Children are obsessed with *getting* from God—getting forgiveness, "Blessed assurance, Jesus is mine," that sense of God having forgiven us our sins— *being* born again. Young adults are obsessed with *doing,* with accomplishment, busyness, achieving something for the kingdom of God. Grandparents, however, are noted for being—for knowing God.

These characteristics described by John demonstrate the best role of the grandparent in the spiritual scheme of things. Perhaps that is why many children find their grandparents easier to relate to on spiritual levels than they do their parents. Parents are busy doing, earning a living, accomplishing—they're goal-oriented. Industry demands a great deal from them; they can be preoccupied. They have tasks to do, goals to achieve, and schedules to meet. This is more true today than it has ever been. Maintenance of today's lifestyle requires great effort—by both parents.

Grandparents, however, are interested in *being,* in knowing God. The grandparents represent the incarnational aspects of the gospel to their grandchildren. Virtually all grandparents notice that they do better with grandchildren than they did with their own children. We're apt to say that the grandchildren are made of better stuff—that's why we brag about them so much, etc. On sober reflection, however, we know that it really has more to do with what we've become as we've matured as human beings in Christ.

LAYING DOWN OUR LIVES

By the time parents have lived and raised children, accomplished their goals, and become grandparents, they have begun to accept the role of *being,* and they are able to lay aside their own needs for the sake of their grandchildren. Jesus tells us that if we save our lives, we lose them, but if we lose our lives for his sake and the gospel, we gain them. Paul says, "I am crucified with Christ, nevertheless I live." Grandparents who love Christ and live in faith have the opportunity to present that truth in an intensely practical and convincing way.

All children, male and female, are basically self-centered people. Adolescents by definition are self-centered. Our natural state is one of preoccupation with self, the insecurity that makes us want to test ourselves against others to make sure we fit in, make sure we're dressed properly, make sure we have been treated in a just and equitable manner. Self-centeredness has to do with our insecurities and fears. We want to make sure we have time for ourselves and space for ourselves. We fear rejection.

As we mature, however, we gradually leave behind both the insecurity and the fear—with the help of God. A mother learns to put the needs of her helpless infant before her own. A father strives to balance his job responsibilities with his desire for time with his wife and family. Parents sacrifice some of their own time and energy and money to help their children grow to responsible adulthood.

ح

Through a lifetime we develop a kind of maturity that comes only when people give up the "me first" mentality and begin to serve others.

Through a lifetime we develop a kind of maturity that comes only when people give up the "me first" mentality and begin to serve others. The promise of God contends that when we die to self or seek the well-being of others, we are rewarded—we gain our lives by losing them.

This maturity, this poise the grandparent gains over a lifetime of practical applied lessons, must be passed on to young people. It does not come naturally or without pain or struggle. Some people go to their graves caught in the same cage of selfishness they lived in as a child. Childlikeness is a biblical virtue, but childishness is a state of retarded development. Grandparents model this principle to grandchildren each time they postpone their own gratification and seek the larger good, whenever they sublimate their will to the will of God or serve others without hope of personal reward.

This does not mean, of course, that grandparents are to be doormats for their children and grandchildren, or that they should allow themselves to be manipulated by other people's desires. True "death to self" has *God* as its focus, not the demands of others. When we submit ourselves fully to God, the Spirit will give us the discernment we need in relating to those around us and serving their needs.

A friend shared this example with me. "We had an adopted grandma who was more like a grandma to us than our own. My real grandmother was very controlling and not very giving and loving. Our adopted grandmother rented a house near my folks and gladly babysat for us when needed. She brought over fresh made donuts, cookies, apple dumplings, and coffee cakes. She taught us to sew, knit, and cook. Sometimes I wonder if there are any people like her left in the world."

"Everyone seems so self-centered and selfish," my friend went on. "As a result of her example we've decided to live close, to encourage our own children to know their grandparents in a different way than we knew ours. I think they need a sense of roots to know a little better who they are themselves. We would be better able to pursue our plans and our careers if we moved to a bigger city, but that's not where our priorities lie. Some people feel we're giving up too much of ourselves by putting in so much effort with our grandchildren, but we see it differently. We're leaving some of ourselves in them, and we think that's important."

THE LARGER PACKAGE

An old proverb says, "A person wrapped up in himself makes a small package." But how will our grandchildren develop a desire to love and care for others?

They might gain it through the same experience base that the grandparents gained it, but there's no guarantee that this will happen. The Bible tells us to "cast our bread on the water." We offer our lives with the hope that something good will result.

A selfless life stands out in a world preoccupied with self-gratification. Mother Teresa is perhaps the most powerful moral influence in the world today, precisely because she has chosen to take Christ at his word and obey. The lessons of self-sacrifice are passed on to grandchildren by grandparents who have taken the gospel message seriously. In this case, the medium is truly the message.

❧

A selfless life stands out in a world preoccupied with self-gratification.

1. The lesson of patience. When I was barely old enough to carry a shotgun, I went hunting with an uncle who was already old—or so it seemed to me. We arrived at the farm to hunt rabbits, and I was out of the car, gun loaded, jacket unzipped, heading across the field, kicking every bush, looking for rabbits. Uncle Chester got out of the car, slowly buckled his boots, got his shotgun loaded, got himself situated and positioned for hunting... he seemed to take an eternity just to get out of the car and get moving. I was two hundred yards out in the field before he actually got away from the car bumper.

I saw him walk into the orchard, slowly moving from tree to tree, and suddenly I heard the crack of a shotgun. Within the next few minutes I heard it again, and he had only covered an eighth of an acre. I had covered twenty acres in the same period. But he had a couple of rabbits, and I had had some exercise! I began to learn that results don't always come from being in a hurry. Certain things are worth waiting for. Freud defined maturity as the ability to postpone gratification.

A child can learn this from grandparents while fishing or hunting, baking cookies, tending a garden, raising chickens—almost any activity except sitting in front of a TV, half asleep. A child wants to thrash around, throw the line out, reel it back in—the sheer joy of the business of cranking the reel is a delight to a grandchild. But when our grandchildren observe our willingness to sit and wait it out, they see that patience catches the fish. They begin to learn then that there are some things worth waiting for in life.

2. The lesson of compassion. Most boys and girls like to step on ants. But my friend Billy and I had refined the ant-squashing business with technology. We found an old electric hotplate in a neighbor's trash barrel, we took it into our garage, and plugged it in. Then we caught ants and put them in the middle of the hotplate so we could watch them run toward the edge before their legs burned off.

When Grandpa discovered us, he was understandably upset—not just because of the dead ants, but because we were getting so much pleasure out of another creature's pain. He said a few words about never torturing anything, but then in his wisdom took us out in the alley and pointed out an ant hill. He got down on one knee and showed us how they were carrying bread in an organized manner, one after the other, down into the hole. He pointed out a conflict that had developed between big black ants and smaller red ants over a bread crust. He patiently explained about the queen ant way down in the hole and the role of the workers and the soldiers. Through his eyes, we discovered the value of watching and learning from ants rather than the short-term pleasure of burning off their legs.

Over the years I have worked with delinquent teenagers. One actually tortured an old wino to death behind a building; another stomped a filling station attendant, the age of his grandfather, to death. I remember my grandfather's lessons of compassion, and I wonder how their lives might have been different if they had had a grandfather take the time to teach them about respect for life.

3. The lesson of frugality. My grandfather took the time to interest me, my sisters, and the neighborhood kids in the deeper things. He was not actually concerned with science, but rather with the meaning of life itself—a sort of living version of "all creatures great and small."

Grandpa had learned the value of making do, of not being totally committed to being a consumer. He took care of his car, his lawn mower, his old jacket, his boots. He didn't need new things when the old things worked just fine.

Grandpa's lawnmower lasts longer than Dad's because Grandpa takes care of his. Eventually, after Daddy has bought several, he'll begin to take care of his as well.

These are the lessons of life and maturity that grand-parents begin to pass on and these are extremely important lessons for young people to learn.

Many grandparents are the first to teach their grand-children the lessons of frugality. Many children start their first bank account with a savings bond or a check that Grandpa or Grandma has given to start them on a path to a lifetime of saving. Virtually all parents want to accomplish the same purpose, but it becomes extremely difficult when they are trying to buy tennis shoes and put food on the table. Grandparents can begin to impart lessons of maturity and the value of saving by helping their grandchildren put a small amount away each week or month and watch it grow. A quarter in a bank each week will teach the lesson and may set a pattern.

4. The lesson of self-reliance. Every grandparent has faced the crisis, usually accompanied with whining and tears, of bored granddaughters and bored grandsons who are staying over at Grandma's and Grandpa's house. "My toys aren't here. Do you have Nintendo? I want to play video games. Where are the tapes for the VCR?" They want to sit like couch potatoes and enjoy TV.

In retreats, family conferences, seminars in churches, camps, Sunday schools, and PTA organizations, without exception, grandparents speak of their grandchildren's lack of ability to entertain themselves or to amuse themselves for even a few minutes. They either want to sit and watch TV or be amused by an adult who explains, assembles, motivates, and meets their every whim and fancy.

As I hear this over and over I wonder if it was any different in my youth. There was no television, but there was the Saturday matinee at the local theater. My dad had to come and get me one Saturday evening because I had sat through the original "King Kong" movie three times! The kids are not so different, but we have an overload of good things. It's not easy even for adults to make the effort to break away and actually do things with grandchildren. It takes time and it takes effort.

At Thanksgiving this year one of my grandsons was whining his way through an NFL football game. I took him by the three-year-old hand, put his coat and hat and boots on him, and started out across the neighborhood. He stopped crying, told me the color of each passing car, wanted to crawl up a culvert, chased a squirrel, fell down and got his hands dirty (the gloves were in my pocket—he didn't think he needed them), and generally made me glad for the out-of-doors, for little boys, and for God's great idea of grandchildren. It's pretty much a toss-up as to who benefits most when we resist our sedentary tendencies and involve ourselves in children's activities.

We can involve our grandchildren in our activities as well. Gardening or doing laundry, working in the yard, canning or freezing vegetables, building a bookshelf or assembling a model bird—all of these activities can teach our grandchildren self-reliance. When we take time to do creative things with our grandchildren, we carve out a special place in their lives beyond what battery-operated plastic toys can have. We experience bonding.

❧

When we take time to do creative things with our grandchildren, we carve out a special place in their lives.

5. The lesson of prayer. One Saturday morning while attending men's prayer breakfast at the church, I ended up in a prayer group with a group of older men, mostly over seventy. As we sat in our small group and began to pray, I noticed that almost all the prayers of the grandparents were for family. To a great degree they were prayers for their grandchildren.

We cannot overestimate the importance of our grandchildren being regularly brought to God in our prayers. In a lifetime of youth work, I have discovered that—almost without exception—young people who have been in the juvenile justice system and in trouble with the law are ones who do not have parents and grandparents praying for them. Young people who succeed in life are often surrounded by support systems, caring parents, extended family, and grandparents who do care. They care enough to pray for them on a regular basis and to give the opportunities that the parents' priority structure may not provide.

I recently read in the local paper that television newswoman Jane Pauley and her husband Garry Trudeau, the cartoonist, had participated in an anniversary celebration at a little church in Franklin, Indiana. Pauley said that her grandparents had brought her as a small child to that very church, and there she had her first memories of learning about God. She said these were "choice and important memories. In fact, for young people growing up, the more good memories, the better."

ह**ॐ**

*"For young people growing up,
the more good memories, the better."*

As I read the article, I wondered if those grandparents ever had any idea what kind of influence their granddaughter and grandson-in-law would eventually have. One of our country's most important opinion-makers was testifying to the impact of grandparents, getting up on a Sunday morning when the granddaughter was visiting, getting her dressed, and taking her to Sunday school. There she developed memories that were so important to her that in middle life, when her presence at a fundraiser or a speaking engagement could command tens of thousands of dollars, she came to a tiny Indiana church in grateful recognition of the influence of her godly grandparents.

In contrast to Jane Pauley's experience—and mine—some grandparents offer a different kind of example. The headline of our local paper last week read, *"Grandmother Hides Crack Cocaine Under Sleeping Infant."* When the police, tracking down a lead on a drug dealer, broke into the grandmother's apartment, a man ran across the bed in his underwear and dived out a bedroom window. He was later apprehended and arrested. The police found a supply of cocaine under a baby sleeping in the room.

The man, apparently, was the father of the sleeping infant; the grandmother in the headline was the mother of his girlfriend, the child's mother. The grandmother was a cocaine user and partner of her son-in-law who was a small-time drug dealer.

Perhaps we should at least be grateful that the grandmother was caring for the baby while her daughter was at work, but I wondered when I read this article what sort of lessons will be transmitted to this baby about life's values, spiritual content, and social responsibility.

What we are as grandparents in the mundane, non-heroic days of our lives, speaks a profound message to watching grandchildren. Babies who sleep on Grand mother's crack cocaine have little foundation for a stable, productive life.

6. The lessons of faith. Some look back to yesteryear and feel that grandparents could have greater impact then. Perhaps in some cases this is true, but the deep needs of today's society make the impact of grandparents even more significant. The Apostle Paul spoke of the early church as shining "like stars in the universe as you hold out the word of life" (Phil 2:15). In today's darkness, spiritual and moral character shine even brighter.

ç**a**

Grandparents can be the conduit through which expressions of faith can come to young people.

Thus, our opportunities as today's grandparents are greater than they have even been. Christian publishers have provided a great resource in the availability of books and tapes for us to use with our grandchildren. There are some truly fine books for children available at the local Christian bookstore. They are not boring books or preachy books; they are not the kind of contrived religious literature that we remember when this genre was first introduced. Skilled people with sophisticated backgrounds in child development have produced books of great value for grandparents to use with their grandchildren.

Janie and I have watched the development of these materials over the years and have developed a great sense of confidence in what they can accomplish. Dr. V. Gilbert Beers, the father of the "Muffin" family from

Moody Press has been called the "Evangelical Dr. Seuss." He has produced children's books that truly have children's interest at heart. This man with two earned doctorates limited himself to the vocabulary of a third grader for six months at a time while he wrote books they could understand in order to communicate Christian faith and values. Our own daughter spent Sunday afternoons in his home with other small children while he read chapters to them and asked for their input, to make sure they were hearing the story and getting the message clearly.

Ken Taylor (of Living Bible fame) participated in the production of the "McGee and Me" video series. I tested these on my own grandchildren; the videos not only had high production value and could compete with anything else being shown on video, but they communicated solid, biblically-based values in interesting stories for young people.

Grandparents can be the conduit through which these expressions of faith can come to young people. Rather than emulating mutant ninja turtles our young people can be entertained—and taught—by selected Christian literature. If parents are unable to supply tapes and books, sometimes grandparents can do it.

The grandparent may also understand, for instance, the value of a week at camp and be able to offer encouragement to their grandchildren's faith in that form. My son is director of a camp for inner-city children, many of whom are able to attend because loving grandparents take the time to sign them up and get them on the bus. The camp is free, but it takes a caring adult to make the hookup. Often Christian young people tell me of finding Christ in a retreat or Bible camp experience, all because someone made it possible for them to attend and be a part of such a program. Such investments by grandparents can have eternal and lasting value.

FILLING IN THE GAPS

My grandfather lived in our home when I was a small boy. When I was seven or eight years old, he took me by the hand and walked me the seven or eight blocks to the Gospel Center Church in South Bend, Indiana, where I attended my first Bible school.

The experience of Grandpa walking me there, and finding him waiting outside the church at the end of Bible school each day, left a lasting impression. I didn't think of it in terms of sacrifice, and it didn't dawn on me that Grandpa would want to do anything else but walk those eight blocks twice a day to be sure I went to Bible school, but it is one of the fondest and warmest memories I have of him.

In the meantime, my dad was struggling to earn a living. He went to the factory every morning and didn't get home until late afternoon. He couldn't possibly have walked me there. Mother did not have a car, and she was occupied with a baby. Grandpa filled in the gaps.

One of my playmates at about this same time had a grandmother who often took care of him. His grandmother would take us to the movies and then she would go to a bingo parlor across the street to play bingo.

After the movie we walked over to the bingo parlor and met her so she could take us home. I can remember sitting on the floor with my friend beside her table, tearing the paper off the cigarette butts that overflowed from the ash trays on the bingo tables. We would then take the pile of tobacco we collected and roll cigarettes with a machine that was available for the convenience of women who wanted to roll their own cigarettes. We sat beneath the thick blue cloud of smoke waiting for his grandmother to take us home, amusing ourselves until the bingo parlor closed.

I don't question that my friend's grandmother was loving and that she cared for him. She did keep both of us from dangers in the night and from the traffic. What she *didn't* do is leave much of an example to a grandson of what the mature Christian ought to be.

❧

We cannot give our grandchildren something which we do not possess. A life thoroughly committed to Christ, lived and tested over time, seasoned with experience and humility, is more powerful than most people ever imagine.

And ultimately, there is a truth in the story that cannot be refuted: we cannot give our grandchildren something which we do not possess. A life thoroughly committed to Christ, lived and tested over time, seasoned with experience and humility, is more powerful than most people ever imagine. Our backgrounds do affect us; we are the product of the blood in our veins. People who have a heritage of godly grandparents carry this influence into their lives sometimes without ever recognizing its source.

When we speak of grandfathers and grandmothers knowing God or putting their emphasis on being like Christ, we are speaking of what theologians call the incarnational principle. It's one thing to talk about God; it's another thing to relate to other people in a responsible and godly manner. But it's even a deeper thing to *be like Jesus Christ,* to flesh out the gospel. This is the ideal toward which we aim our lives as we face the prospect of being good grandparents.

In a day where youth is almost idolized and where productivity is considered the only measurement of worth, it is valuable to remind ourselves of how God has programmed the natural world. The blossom on the flower is prized, photographed, sold in bouquets, and noticed by everyone. But in the real scheme of things, the blossom performs the function of attracting the bee which carries the pollen for the purpose of producing the seed. In old age we may not be much of a blossom, but we are the seed. It is the goal toward which human existence aims.

❧

In old age we may not be much of a blossom, but we are the seed.

A peach is not produced by a peach tree in order to be eaten by a passerby. The real purpose of the peach is to surround the seed, to provide the seed with the nutrients and moisture that it needs to sprout another peach tree. In biblical terms, the fruit of the Spirit is the character of Christ—"love, joy, peace, patience, kindness, goodness, faithfulness, gentleness, and self-control" (Gal 5:22). This maturity regenerates the Christian faith as it surrounds the seed of our life, planted in the soil of our families. When we live the life of Christ with our families and our grandchildren, we plant the seed of a new and brighter future.

SEVEN

The Spittin' Image

I GREW UP HEARING people say, "He's the spittin' image of his father." Speculation has it that the phrase comes from people in America copying the language of the Scotsman. The Scotsman has a burr in his speech and trills his Rs. When the Scots referred to a boy, they often said he was "the spirit and image of his father." But to the untrained ear, "the spirit and image of his father" sounded like "spittin' image." The phrase essentially meant, "Inside and out, he's just like his dad."

ક્ષ

This is our ultimate destiny in Christ—to be the "spirit and image" of our Heavenly Father.

This is our ultimate destiny in Christ—to be the "spirit and image" of our Heavenly Father. But to take on that image, we need to have some idea of his spirit and image—what God "looks like," what his character is. One way we get that is from our parents and grandparents.

ROOTS

Part of the role of parents and grandparents is to pass on things from generation to generation. One of the most direct passages in the entire Scripture speaking about the role of the generations is found in Deuteronomy 6:

> Hear O, Israel: the Lord our God, the Lord is one. Love the Lord your God with all your heart and with all your soul and with all your strength. These commandments that I give you today are to be upon your hearts. Impress them on your children. Talk about them when you sit at home and when you walk along the road, when you lie down and when you get up. Tie them as symbols on your hands and bind them on your foreheads. Write them on the doorframes of your houses and on your gates.

These "commandments" center on the Ten Commandments, of course, but they're surrounded by a myriad of laws and patterns the people of God were supposed to follow. As we read further in the Old Testament we even find instruction about diet and preparation of food and all sorts of things that have to do with ordinary living. We may find all this detail a bit tedious, but God's purpose was to give his people a pattern for living that they could pass on to future generations.

The powerful film *On Golden Pond* dealt with the impact grandparents can provide in situations of pain in family life. In the story, a confused, hurting boy is withdrawing from his family. His protective cynicism and indifference push away those who love him. He is frighteningly typical of dozens of kids we have worked with over the years.

As the story unfolds, the boy is dropped off, trapped with his aging grandparents for the summer. He observes their interaction, their relationship, their love, their impatience with each other, their territoriality, their struggles and frailties. He is preoccupied with his own problems and does not want to be distracted from wallowing in his own misery.

Then, slowly trust begins to develop between the grandson and grandparents. He begins to refocus his life, turning from himself to concern for his grandfather.

As grandparents, part of our task is to make sure that the essential principles of our lives and values are passed on meaningfully through our grandchildren. Some of these are issues of faith and morality; others are cultural traditions. Grandparents can be instrumental in helping parents teach young people those things which make up a meaningful life, the connectors that hold together our family's national story and history.

❧

As grandparents, part of our task is to make sure that the essential principles of our lives and values are passed on meaningfully through our grandchildren.

A few years ago a series of books were published, entitled *The Foxfire Books*. These books were created when a teacher was trying to teach Appalachian mountain children in the schoolroom and found that they felt the classroom curriculum was irrelevant to their lives. They lived practical lives on small rocky farms and couldn't quite see how readin', writin', and 'rithmetic really applied. In order to teach the young people the research and investigation skills they needed, she sent them out around the mountain communities to interview the old people—especially grandparents—about the mountain crafts, folklore, and their way of life.

After interviewing the older people the children wrote about what they learned. These books are a kind of chronicle of grandparents' wisdom. Including such fascinating subjects as how to pluck a chicken, how to make a bark basket, how to butcher a hog, and how to make lard, the books ignited interest in rural America and made the children very proud of their forebears. Their education began to come alive as they learned the way that their lives were connected to their real world.

I remember when my son read *The Foxfire Books*. He came to me one day after a large oak tree had blown down in our yard during a storm and said, "Dad, what are we going to do with that oak tree?"

"Well, we'll probably have to cut it up and make it into firewood," I said, "because I don't know what else to do with it. It probably has some good wood in it, but I don't know who to go to get it made into lumber. Sawmills usually won't cut trees from a yard."

"I have an idea," he replied. "Let's make a split rail fence around our woods."

"Son, there's a lot of work involved in doing this," I said.

"Well, I've got this book that tells about it."

"Let's read the book," I said.

The book described how to split logs with wedges and sledge hammer. My son had read about Abraham Lincoln being a logsplitter and thought that maybe we would appreciate Abe even more after the effort.

The trunk was about forty feet long to the first limb, and then a good deal of large limb wood. We spent that entire winter splitting this tree into oak rails. One day he said to me, "Dad, do you suppose we're the only people in West Chicago who are making a hand-split, oak, rail fence?"

"I'd be willing to bet on it!" I said.

Later he said, "Do you suppose we're the only people in Illinois making a handsplit, oak, rail fence?" He kept this up until he decided we were doing something that was unique in the entire universe that particular winter— with a maul and wedges making a fence out of split oak.

TOUCHING THE PAST

We could have built the fence more cheaply, and with a lot less work if we had bought the split rails at a lumber yard. But carrying on the process with him, however, deepened our father/son relationship. Now he seems interested in doing this same sort of thing with his boys— building a tree house, making it out of logs, going about it in the "old-fashioned" way so that he can teach them a little bit about what it means that Abe Lincoln split logs. It dawned on me that my father did the same thing with me; I have always felt a certain sense of self-reliance because my father taught me skills that were out of date and no longer practiced in this society.

That knowledge and those skills have given me a sense of connection with my own roots. I know what a threshing machine does. I have built fences for livestock, shingled a roof, and assisted in butchering animals. I have dug a well. I have helped my father build several houses with our own hands.

These things are not really important in themselves. But they speak of the connectedness with past generations. I go fishing with my dad's fishing tackle and have memories connected with each of the lures, the lessons that he taught me in the boat. My son has fished with the same lures, and now our grandchildren are using them as well. They carry the name of Kesler, the name has meaning to them because they are able to feel and touch the past.

A good friend of mine teaches history at a state college. Paul is an outstanding authority on the Civil War and collects Civil War memorabilia. I invited him to lecture at Taylor University during the Interterm last January in a section on the Civil War. The students had recently seen the Civil War movie, *Glory,* featuring a black regiment and their preparation for battle.

In the movie there is a very moving scene the night before the battle. The black soldiers had gathered around the campfire having a prayer meeting before entering into combat. They were praying for courage, that they would represent the North well, and most of all they were concerned that they would prove to white soldiers that black soldiers were men of valor and could indeed carry out their military assignments.

Part of the service was a scene in which the men sang while being accompanied by a tambourine. Paul actually had acquired a Civil War tambourine with the very identification markings of that particular black regiment on it. He asked the students how many had seen the film, and they sleepily held up their hands and said they had. He then reminded them of the scene that I mentioned and then asked if they would like to touch that scene. He reached into his briefcase and pulled out this tambourine and passed it around the room. Each student touched it and handed it to the next person. Suddenly the atmosphere in the room changed from boredom to rapt attention. Tears began to drip off the cheeks of the students as they actually touched the past and touched this scene. Paul went on to explain that this might not be the exact tambourine, and he was not altogether sure that the scene depicted in the film actually took place, but he did know that this tambourine belonged to that very regiment and all those men had died in that battle. The students, actually feeling history, experienced it at a different level than they would have experienced it otherwise.

Grandparents can help grandchildren touch their roots, touch meaning, understand the lessons of the generations. And they can help them understand their importance to God and the importance of carrying on the valuable things of civilization.

I believe this is part of what grandparents can do for young people. We help them touch their roots, touch meaning, understand the lessons of the generations. And as a result of having that sense of position—where they are in human history—they can understand their importance to God and the importance of carrying on the valuable things of civilization.

Carving on the casket. Laverne Atha, the father of a college friend, was a man much like Atticus in the play, *To Kill A Mockingbird*. He was a lawyer, a solid Christian leader, a protector of the weak and poor, a flower gardener with acres of peonies. But above all, he was a man of character and integrity.

Laverne Atha had a sense of humor unmatched by anyone I've ever known. He went to church in his navy suit, impeccably pressed, with his curly thick white hair combed into place. He always looked like a prophet would have looked if he had lived in the twentieth century. But before going to church on one particular day, he took a needle and white thread and ran a long piece of white thread through the back shoulder seam of his suit coat. He kept the spool of thread intact and put it in his pocket.

He sat down in church in front of a fastidious lady and waited for her to see the white thread. Then, during the prayer, he felt a tug on the string. He just fed her more thread until she had about a yard of it in her hand. He then felt her break the thread and shift nervously in her pew, probably waiting for his sleeve to fall off!

Mr. and Mrs. Atha were doting grandparents who involved their grandchildren in all of their family's activities. When LaVerne died, his son, Grayson, a pastor, officiated at his funeral. They gathered at the graveside looking at the fine wood coffin. The grandchildren were deeply grieved, and some of them were inconsolable. Grayson saw the plight of the grandchildren and walked over to the pile of dirt hidden beneath the fake grass. He found a stone, then walked up to the casket and scratched a cross into the impeccable finish of the casket. "When I think of my dad, I think of Jesus, and so I made a cross," he said. "What do you think of when you think of grandpa? What would you like to say to him?" One of the grandsons took the stone and wrote, *I love you.* One by one they carved their messages on the lid of the casket.

When I heard this story I thought, first, that LaVerne must be laughing uproariously at the shock many people would have over "defilement" of an expensive coffin even if it was to be buried anyway. Then I hoped that he knew the deep impact he had made on his grandchildren and how deeply they wanted to preserve his influence. They wrote on his casket; he wrote on their hearts and lives and he has written on mine.

BECOMING CONSERVATIONISTS

Someone has wisely said we become conservative when we have something to conserve. The memory of LaVerne Atha is worth conserving. Many people today feel they have nothing of value to conserve. They don't want to pass it on to their children because their own lives have been so confused and so empty and so meaningless. But those of us who have experienced God through Jesus Christ and have, through his power in our lives, experienced the love of family, can perform a valuable service to our culture, to our grandchildren, and to God himself, by presenting to them a pattern to follow. It is not a violation of humility to try to make an impact and to desire that it be preserved.

The Apostle Paul, you remember, was not afraid to tell people to imitate him. He was an imitator of Christ; others should imitate his imitation of Christ. Godly grandparents can do the same. Indeed, this is not just an opportunity or a privilege, but a mandate from God as expressed in the Deuteronomy 6 passage.

A goal of each of us as believers is to be the "spirit and image" of the Son of God, Jesus Christ. Through the process of grandparenting, we want our grandchildren to be the spirit and image they've learned from us. Through this generational process the truly valuable things are passed on from one generation to the next.

❧

The godliness we attempt to build into our lives is expressed in practical human situations—trustworthiness, knowledge, dependability, patience. All the "fathers" of our faith are not just ancient men and women who lived centuries ago. We have the responsibility to be "fathers" today for the benefit of our grandchildren and succeeding generations.

God has revealed himself to us as Heavenly Father. "Our father which art in heaven" was written in a period in history when the father was the oldest male living in the particular clan or family group. When we speak of the *fathers* in the Bible, we don't speak of just the parent, we speak of those with whom our welfare is entrusted. Young people have quite a lot of struggle thinking of God in terms of their thirty-five-year-old parents. They more often think of God as being like their fifty-or sixty-year-old grandparents or eighty-year-old great-grandparents. This is not inconsistent with intent of the Scripture. The godliness we attempt to build into our lives is expressed in practical human situations—trustworthiness, knowledge, dependability, patience. The fruit of the Spirit reflects the "spirit and image" of our Father. All the "fathers" of our faith are not just ancient men and women who lived centuries ago—Augustine, Polycarp, Wesley,

Calvin, and others. *We* have the responsibility to be "fathers" today for the benefit of our grandchildren and succeeding generations.

For many years in the Youth for Christ ministry, we have been involved with young people, especially in direct evangelism. Over the years, as society has seemingly developed more cracks, the energies of the staff have been aimed at unchurched youth, those who somehow have been untouched by organized Christian effort. As a result of this concern, a trust relationship has developed between many juvenile judges, social workers, police, probation officers, and YFC staff. The strategy that evolved was to develop relationships with troubled, neglected and delinquent youth on the streets. We took to the streets. We learned to hang out with them and to develop friendships. This is still a major part of the Youth for Christ effort worldwide.

Most of the staff were educated in Christian colleges and seminaries and took the prescribed courses in biblical languages and study of the Scriptures, as well as sociology and psychology. We would take these kids—mostly boys in those days—away to camps, and after spending many hours playing softball and volleyball, swimming, hiking, mountain climbing, and canoeing, we would try to communicate the gospel to them with the aim of seeing them commit their lives to Christ. Our philosophy was basically that "the heart of the problem is the heart of the delinquent."

We shared the biblical story of God's love for them. We told them, "God loves you. He is your Heavenly Father. He sent his Son, Jesus, to the earth to communicate his love." These ideas of God, the Creator, being a "heavenly Father" are supposed to evoke feelings of security and comfort. But with these kids, the very words that were supposed to engender trust and openness brought fear.

Suddenly it dawned on us. Who is a father to these boys? What is he like? He comes home drunk, abuses his wife, slaps the boy around, intimidates the whole family and then falls asleep in his own vomit. No wonder the boys would fear a heavenly Father who, in addition to being cruel, is all powerful—you can't hide from him and he knows everything.

We discovered that for a whole segment of today's youth, the proper idea of "father" was missing. Kids need elders, male and female, to fulfill this role—not simply to function as a parent functions, but to be, to incarnate, to flesh out the qualities of God. Grandparents can fulfill that need—they can represent Christ to their grandchildren, and thus perpetuate the values of the Scripture.

EIGHT

Building Memories

W HEN PEOPLE DECIDE to sell cookies, breads, pies, cakes, and other commercial products, they often label them "Grandma's Homemade Cookies" or "Grandma's Pies." One of the funniest cartoons I ever remember seeing was a picture of a huge factory labeled "Grandma's Home Baked Pies" with great smokestacks belching out steam and smoke. In a cutaway in the corner of the picture, a little grandma, wearing an apron, with her hair in a bun, was sweating profusely, putting out pies—the only worker in this great factory, with dozens of trucks lined up to haul them all away.

In our sophisticated modern culture, of course, we know that most things with grandma's name on them were produced by some great, groaning, belching machine and not grandma at all. The sentiment we reach for in this advertising is the sense of well-being, an "over the river and through the woods, to grandmother's house we go," kind of security. In modern culture, this is a difficult ideal to preserve, especially since we don't go over the river, in a sleigh any more. We go down an expressway through a toll booth, across a bridge, down another highway to a brick building, where we stick a piece of plastic into a machine that talks in a mechanical voice and allows us into grandma's condo, where we take an elevator to her apartment and she throws something into a microwave. This is a very different world.

෭෧

Even the most cynical and jaded young people are brought back to a reevaluation of their values and life directions in the midst of these family traditions. Grandparents are the centerpieces of these memories.

TRADITION!

Most young people today live in a world that is very much like a movie set. Nothing is permanent; everything is a sham. There are very few things we can put our faith in. Pop heroes and rock stars are here today and gone tomorrow. Fashions change with every season and whim. In the midst of all of this change and the uncertainties surrounding it, the sights and smells of grandma's house are a stabilizing and important influence. Even the most cynical and jaded young people are brought back to a reevaluation of their values and life directions in the midst of these family traditions. Grandparents are the centerpieces of these memories.

Perhaps this accounts for the popularity and timelessness of the play, *Fiddler on the Roof.* The word *tradition,* conjures up a mental picture of the fiddler on the roof, where lives are so unsure, so filled with pain, poverty, injustice, and ambiguity that they need traditions to hold them steady. Though we do not live in czarist Russia, we know we also need something to hold us steady, something to keep us from falling off our roofs.

Worldwide wars and conflicts rage over cultural identity. Each warring group has a history, an identity, a culture and traditions that bind them together and give them continuity. Are these differences worth fighting and dying for? How can we celebrate ethnicity and still maintain civility within the world?

The people fighting for their cultural identity know that no culture can survive long or maintain its identity without its rituals and its traditions. The prospect of losing these symbols and being amalgamated into some faceless structure seems worse than death—and given some of the alternatives, they may be right.

America has long been committed to the development of a *new* culture forged in the melting pot of many blended ethnicities. We have developed national rituals and traditions such as the fourth of July, Thanksgiving, and Memorial Day to maintain our unity. Ethnic groups within the culture have tried to maintain their own holidays and celebrations to remember their heritage while being part of the larger whole—such as St. Patrick's Day in the Irish community.

Several years ago we were attempting to make inroads into the Hispanic community in the Chicago area. We had established contact with the kids, most of whom were the sons and daughters of established Hispanic-American families who had come to the United States in the 1920s to build railroads. They ended up establishing homes and were a visible part of the community, but there was little contact with them other than at school.

To my surprise, many of the teenage girls were unable to attend our Campus Life meetings because of the concern of their grandmothers. I met with them, and in no uncertain terms these grandmothers complained to me that in their eyes the greatest problem in American culture was that girls were allowed to go out on dates and attend parties and dances without chaperons. They explained that the role of grandparents, especially grandmothers, was to protect the purity of young women. Even though our purposes were pure and we were Christians, under no circumstances were they going to allow this part of their culture to be compromised.

I left the meeting feeling that I had a great deal to learn about Hispanic family life and the strength of those extended families.

At present a national debate of some consequence is raging over the issue of pluralism—whether we can maintain our ethnic distinctives and still maintain national unity. Some feel that the ideal of national identity is no longer viable or even desirable. They seek for assurances and protections under the law for the rights and entitlements of their own ethnicities. Others see even this as too confining and seek personal, individualistic identity, desiring to function as individuals with no sense of loyalty or obligation to any group, even the family.

૨૦

We need to restore the values, loyalties, and security of family life to provide an environment in which children can grow up safe and healthy to become what God intended them to be.

Christians, observing this fragmentation and the breakdown of the family unit at both the nuclear and extended level, search for ways to "put this Humpty Dumpty back together again." We need to restore the values, loyalties, and security of family life to provide an environment in which children can grow up safe and healthy to become what God intended them to be.

Maintaining family ties. Families, like all other cultural units, maintain their cohesiveness through social commitments solemnized through ceremony, ritual and tradition.

Generations of human beings have been able to mark the really valuable things in life in terms of the smells, foods, rituals, decorations, and pleasant sensations attached to family holidays, national observations, and religious festivals. Our Christian traditions provide additional opportunities that are not only rich in family memories, but that tie us as well to God and to our faith.

Our Christian calendar begins with the birth of the Savior. Almost all grandparents have a conversation every year or two about whether or not they should take the effort to get the Christmas decorations out and decorate the house—after all, it's only the two of them. But then they think about that one day when the family does come, when the kids look at, touch, and fondle the familiar decorations—the street scene with lights, the special angels, the bells, the manger scene, the family homemade ornaments that are timeworn and laughable. Suddenly we realize we are part of something a little larger than we can understand.

With blended families, in-laws, and the complexities of modern life, it's easy to simply give in to a sort of business-as-usual schedule, where we allow some restaurant or department store to provide the energy for our celebrations. Sometimes it doesn't seem worth the effort. Life is simply too complicated.

But in our family we've found that it is worth the effort to put a little more into it. Our entire family gathers for Christmas together—children and all the grandchildren. We aren't always able to do it on December 25, because there are other family considerations and other grandparents to consider, but our part is to try to provide our memories as best we can, in the hopes that our grandchildren will be surrounded with a wonderful sense of love, family values, and stability—things worth conserving in their lives and in their children's children.

One of my roles is to be the first one up on Christmas morning. I start a fire in the fireplace and then I get out my cowbell—a loud bell I purchased in Switzerland years ago that used to hang on someone's family milk cow. My own children remember being awakened by that bell when they were small children themselves. I wander through the house ringing this bell and believe me, its sound is loud and startling enough that being awakened by it makes Christmas different from any other day in the entire year. The young children usually cry when they hear it for the first time. When they are big and brave and older, they tell the little ones to be ready, because Grandpa is going to startle them early on Christmas morning with his cowbell. "Grandpa, are you going to wake us with the cowbell?" It provides a great sense of anticipation, just a little fear, and a little nonsense that makes Christmas special.

On Christmas Eve we all gather around the Christmas tree and sing carols together. We share the Christmas story, reading from the Bible about "swaddling clothes" and "the babe lying in a manger," and we also have some fun reading once again about the "little old driver so lively and quick, I knew in a moment it must be St. Nick."

Within two or three years, all our grandchildren have feelings of warmth permanently etched in their minds— the sense of being surrounded by love, the feel of flannel pajamas, the sensation of grandma's beds and the way they smell, the scent of good things being cooked in the kitchen to be eaten later. They begin to enjoy the anticipation, the presents that are wrapped and the surprises inside, the fun things and things not so fun—like saying "thank you" for clothes, even when you don't quite mean it; like being glad when you get something with a battery in it.

We deal with tears and broken toys, with understanding that someone got something that you didn't get; yet you got something that almost compensated. Together we learn the lessons of life and family and of being loved, of belonging.

And we're especially happy at this stage that great-grandma Kesler is always there. The grandchildren call her Grandma K and she enjoys her special place. We're able to teach respect for her family, her contribution, her age, and her wisdom, and the grandchildren are encouraged to approach her, not with familiarity, but with that sense of awe that belongs to her generation. Besides that, she's a lot of fun. She's patient, she's able to soothe feelings better than most, and when someone really feels a need to be understood, a short time in her lap can solve virtually any child's problem.

The meaning of little things. Our extended family, I realize, is the exception rather than the rule. We live in a world where industry demands mobility, where the typical forty-year-old father moves every three years. Developing family traditions can be difficult, but a tradition does not have to be a full blown Labor Day Parade to have meaning.

I will never forget my fourth grade teacher, Madge E. Allen, who told us, "I am like the straits of Magellan (Madge E. Allen)." When she was sixty, she taught me prepositions by crawling *under* the desk, *over* the desk, *around* the desk, *through* the desk, *across* the desk, *behind* the desk, *beside* the desk, until I thoroughly understood, even today, what a preposition is. She understood the importance of tradition and established one with me.

I contracted scarlet fever in the fourth grade and had to be quarantined for several weeks while all of my skin peeled off and grew back again. She stopped by my house two or three times a week to give me my assignments, answer questions and encourage me in my independent study. One day when she came I told her that my birthday was the next week. She came to see me and brought me a birthday card. For the next twenty years, I always received a birthday card from Madge E. Allen until she died. She always addressed it to "Jay Kesler, A Very Special Boy." Her tradition was very important to me while growing up and did make me feel special. I always felt that I had to live up to Miss Allen's trust.

We can do small things to be the Madge E. Allens in our grandchildren's lives—send a note of congratulations on a good report card, for example. Letters are more lasting than phone calls; people often keep them until they are dog-eared, reading them again and again. Several years ago it dawned on me that most teenagers have never received a first-class personal letter from an adult. They receive letters from friends and get advertisements from people selling things, but seldom receive a thoughtful letter. I began writing letters to kids and encouraging parents and grandparents to do the same. And I have been amazed at how powerfully the tradition of a letter on a birthday, Christmas, or the anniversary of a special occasion can be. As one student put it, "My grandfather never misses my birthday. He is sort of a poet and always writes a birthday poem for me and the other grandchildren, mostly about nature and life. I read them over and over. Some day we'll have a collection of these in our family. I think that's pretty special."

Not all of us are poets, but then again, this granddad is probably no Robert Frost, either. What he is, is a grandfather who understands how powerful even small predictabilities—traditions if you please—can be.

ॐ

We can't all be Norman Rockwell families, but we can, within the limitations of our own situation, make a place for personal traditions.

We can't all be Norman Rockwell families, but we can, within the limitations of our own situation, make a place for personal traditions. What we can't live with successfully is the absence of caring others.

Each family does it differently and each family has its own traditions. But whatever the traditions, children raised in families are more fortunate than children raised without them. The sad truth is, through a combination of the breakdown of the home in America and the busy life and complications involved in attempting to build families out of family fragments, more and more children are being raised without these traditions. We will pay a terrible price for the loss of these traditions. And we don't have to pay a great price—in financial terms—to build memories and traditions with our grandchildren. Eggs are cheap. To color two or three dozen eggs with Grandma and Grandpa can provide a great evening of togetherness. When kids wake in the morning to find those eggs and others made of chocolate and candies hidden around through the house or—if the weather permits—outside, they will always remember the fun and excitement of being around their grandparents. An Easter egg hunt does not require a country estate; it can be done in a single room in a nursing home. It may not compete with Disney World, but grandchildren remember and want to come visit again.

Ham at Easter, turkey at Thanksgiving, and barbecue on Christmas are our traditions—yours may be different, but whatever they are, begin them now. Start your "first annual family tradition."

We have had numerous boys from the Youth for Christ group homes share our holidays. Even today, years later, young men will introduce themselves to me and say, "Remember the Thanksgiving day we spent at your mother's home?" Sometimes I do and sometimes I don't, but they do. A holiday meal is a small gesture for such a lasting impression!

I was discussing family traditions with a grandfather in the Bahamas and he told me that he takes all of his granddaughters for a "before breakfast swim" in the ocean near their home every Christmas morning. His house is about the size of a typical American garage, but it is Grandpa's house, and the special swim and Christmas breakfast are things the grandchildren wouldn't miss for the world.

Most grandchildren today have had more ice cream by the time they're six than their great-grandparents had in a lifetime; though we surely are moderns and know our way around the local supermarket, we make ice cream at home with an ice cream freezer. Where else do you get to crank an ice cream freezer but at Grandpa's house? You pour salt over ice, turn the crank, until you're tired but won't admit it, then turn it one last time. Some things seem too simple to have meaning, but experience convinces me of their importance. Grandma and Grandpa can provide these opportunities.

Our kids would say that Grandpa Smith has left them memories that they will never forget, and when they are grandparents they want to be like him. He certainly couldn't afford to give them expensive presents, but what he did give them was time. They helped him find a coffee can and helped him dig garden worms. Then they sat and waited for little blue gills to bite. They helped him clean them, then cooked them and ate them together. The ritual took up a whole day almost every time they visited him. No wonder they couldn't wait to visit Grandpa Smith!

One young lady confessed, "At my grandmother's house we shell peas and lima beans. I guess I always thought that they came frozen from the store!"

"Why are these things important?" I asked.

She said, "Well, it's just important to know that there are things that have always been that you can depend on. You know there's something solid about things that don't change, like growing things and grandmas."

At Grandma's house children can help with things—set the table, fold the napkins, light candles (if they're old enough). They can even help Grandpa light the barbecue if they're big enough and stand back as the thing goes "poof!" At Grandma's house they have their own places at the table; they can stay up late and have popcorn and talk. They can play games without a computer attached, games with lots of pieces, like Monopoly and Sorry. Grandpa doesn't have a Nintendo, but he does have puzzles, and the grandchildren can sit and figure them out forever. What an accomplishment for children to finally get the last piece in place and leave it on the table until Mom and Dad come and see that they've done something their parents did as children. Grandma and Grandpa's house is a place of memories, a place kids can depend on in a world in flux. Grandma may be alone or Grandpa may be in a nursing home, but they are still part of the family to a young person.

In working with delinquent and troubled youth, I've often wondered what makes the difference. Is it because they are poor? Is it racial? Is it the effect of divorce? alcohol? abuse? I see it all with these kids, and yet I also meet kids with these same situations or combinations of factors, kids who never get into trouble, stay in school, and overcome all of the obstacles.

What I do notice in failed homes is a lack of attention to the little things. Everyone seems to have given up. The table is never set, there are no decorations, no handcrafts, no art, nothing to remind people that they are part of something larger than themselves.

ࢀ

Family traditions and efforts to establish identity are necessary to family health.

Family traditions and efforts to establish identity are necessary to family health. Grandparents can often make that contribution in today's culture. If grandparents make the effort, they can provide the difference that may balance the scale in favor of the next generation.

NINE

When Our Children Divorce

IN FAMILY CONFERENCES around the country, I have talked with many grandparents who are struggling with the complexities brought upon them because of divorce. Their struggles often center around one of three sets of circumstances:

1. Their son or daughter has custody of the children, and the grandparent is trying to fill in the gap by giving emotional support to the family and attempting to provide some help or backup.

2. Their son or daughter has custody, but he or she is unable to manage financially. The son or daughter and the grandchildren return home and are living with the parents. During the day, when the parent is off working to keep body and soul together, the grandparents are raising the child as coparents.

3. Their son or daughter has lost custody, and the grandchildren are separated from them by a custodial parent preoccupied with his or her own life. The non-custodial grandparents can be cut out of the life of grandchildren

whom they love very much.

Each of these situations has its own complexities, including the intervention of the legal system. It is impossible to suggest a course of action that will fit each situation but if grandparents can maintain objectivity and resist saying and doing things that further complicate the problem, over time they may be able to restore their place of involvement.

HOLDING THE NET

In one particularly nasty divorce situation, the mother's animosity toward her divorced husband seemed to focus on his mother. She said very unkind and ugly things to her mother-in-law, most of which were unfounded. Her hatred took on an energy of its own, and after the divorce one of her central goals was to move as far away from the grandmother as possible and make it virtually impossible for the grandchildren to have contact with her. The grandmother was heartbroken.

My counsel was that the grandmother not further infuriate the estranged daughter-in-law, but that she write her a letter in which she set the guidelines of her desires for the grandchildren. She promised never to take sides or speak of either parent in a derogatory manner. She asked that her birthday cards and presents be given to the grandchildren. She promised that her gifts would not be lavish or seductive to the grandchildren. The mother reluctantly agreed, but in her return letter, established that she was in charge and that she would decide what was appropriate.

I suggested a letter rather than a phone call because if such confrontations are carried out face to face, the conflicting parties may not possess the self-control, especially during the strain of the divorce battle, to resist escalation and argument. A letter often works better because it can be read and re-read until it says what is intended. In this case, the strained relationship went on for several years. The mother developed a relationship with another man, and when she became ready to remarry, she asked the divorced husband and his family if they would take the children because she was unable to fit them into her new life. I believe that in this case a patient, less aggressive approach by the grandparents paid off for all concerned.

Other situations become more complicated. One grandmother related a deep fear that her grandchildren were in an atmosphere of possible physical danger because of drug parties that were held in their daughter-in-law's apartment. Although the children were supposed to be asleep, she felt that the people and activities that accompanied these parties were not good influences for the grandchildren. She and her husband decided to go to court and attempt to persuade the judge to give them custody.

We have all seen articles and TV exposés of seeming inconsistencies and injustices of the courts in such situations. But in the overwhelming number of cases the courts are seeking justice, fairness and common sense. There are, however, failures. And it takes persistence, considerable money and a great sense of love and responsibility to pursue these cases. These grandparents felt angry, exhausted, and powerless, but nonetheless continued their efforts.

Their story does not yet have an ending. Many of these cases simply continue until a child is actually harmed or a parent becomes institutionalized or dies. In the meantime, the grandparents wait, holding the net to catch the falling child.

When the parents have both become nonfunctional—through drugs, alcohol, or in some cases, death—the grandparents often find themselves with the burden of raising their grandchildren. After so many years, the task is physically and emotionally difficult. Grandparents don't want to see their grandchildren put up for adoption. They love them very much, but are caught in a web of tremendous responsibility and complexity.

As one grandfather put it, "You spend your whole life raising your kids and trying to get them established and then the whole thing gets dumped back on you. We took our daughter to church, provided a good and stable home and got her through college. She married a boy who we thought was fine for her and we loved him very much. He became unsure of himself, lost his self-confidence, lost his job and then seemed to just 'flip out.' He deceived us, lied about his financial dealings, took advantage of us with loans and help, and then just took off. Now we have our daughter and two infants back home. They have debts, and it's a small town, and I feel responsible. It's just a real mess!"

An aged grandmother, probably in her mid-seventies, wanted to discuss her problem. She told me a long story of pain in her own life, how her marriage had ended in divorce and then how her son and daughter-in-law had almost destroyed themselves with alcohol and drugs and had left their son to be raised by her. They had left him with her for an overnight and never returned.

As we talked, a teenager about sixteen years old walked up and asked her a question about an activity he wanted to participate in. She gave permission and then introduced him to me as her grandson. He was polite, respectful and enthusiastic, and I was impressed.

Later I talked with him at some length and discovered that he probably had more insight into his parents and his plight than most therapists would have. He then told me how grateful he was for his grandmother and the fact that they were helping each other. When I inquired about his parents he said, "I pray for them, but I really can't help them. The best thing I can do is get my life on track and leave them to God; otherwise we'll all sink and our whole family will be a disaster. I'm going to be the one exception to the rule in our family so my grandmother will have something to be proud of." There are many stories of success among the disasters; in this case, one rather frail grandmother was making the difference.

The Apostle Paul's young protégé, Timothy, was apparently raised by his grandmother and his mother. His father is not mentioned—according to some biblical scholars, because he is a Greek. But it may well be that Timothy was the product of abandonment. In first century culture, young love often could not sustain itself after the ethnic and religious and racial complications began to take their toll on the marriage relationship. Very likely Timothy was raised by two adults, his mother and his grandmother.

ॐ

Many less than ideal situations begin with sadness but have happy endings when people—like Timothy's grandmother— make themselves available.

Is this a family? Of course it is! Is it the easiest arrangement, or even the ideal? Probably not, but it apparently worked for Timothy. And God added the Apostle Paul as a surrogate father figure. Many less than ideal situations begin with sadness but have happy endings when people — like Timothy's grandmother—make themselves available.

A PORTRAIT OF DIVORCE

Every divorce situation is different, but there are some experiences common to all children of divorce. In all situations of divorce, there is confusion for the children. When two adults think they've solved their problem by divorcing, they have not necessarily made their children's lives less complex. Some people will argue that children raised away from an unhappy home are better off than those raised in a home where there is fighting and squabbling. And certainly, when there is verbal or physical abuse, children sometimes want to escape the parent out of fear.

But I have listened for hundreds of hours to young people tell their stories and they almost always feel that their parents didn't try hard enough to keep their marriage together. Perhaps the most extensive and well-known study of the effects of divorce on children is Wallerstein and Kelley's five year study of sixty divorced families in California. According to the study:

- The initial reaction of over 90 percent of the children was "an acute sense of shock, intense fears, and grieving which the children found overwhelming."
- Half of the children feared being abandoned forever by the parent who had left (a realistic fear in light of other studies that show that within three years after the divorce decree 50 percent of the fathers never see their

children). One-third feared being abandoned by the custodial parent. The children were preoccupied with the fear of waking to find both parents gone.

• Following the divorce, a significant number of children suffered feelings of despondency, rejection, anger and guilt. The researchers report: "Two-thirds of the children, especially the younger children, yearned for the absent parent... with an intensity we found profoundly moving."

• Five years after the divorce, 37 percent of the children were moderately to severely depressed, were intensely unhappy and dissatisfied with their lives. Their unhappiness was greater at five years than it had been at one and a half years after the divorce.

• Ten years after the divorce, 41 percent of the children were doing poorly, "entering adulthood as worried, underachieving, self-deprecating and angry young men and women." Some children showed no symptoms until they were about to enter a close relationship themselves as young adults. Adolescents appear to be most vulnerable to the effects of divorce. Some studies indicate 80 percent to 100 percent of adolescents in inpatient mental hospitals are children of divorce.*

The sobering reality about these observations is that they are not statistics. They are someone's grandchildren.

Millions of children have been raised by grandparents as a result of tragedy, war and death; however, it is a more complex and demanding task when children face

---

* (From *Surviving the Breakup* by Wallerstein and Kelly, New York: Basic Books, 1980 as quoted in the pamphlet "What Do We Know About Successful Families?" by Armand M. Nicholi, Jr., MD, Harvard Medical School, Massachusetts General Hospital.)

abandonment and divorce. Children can accept tragedy; rejection is much harder to accept.

STABILIZING THE SEE-SAW

When they have been victimized by divorce, grandchildren are confused and hurt and often filled with anger, resentment, and guilt that they really don't understand. The role of the grandparent at this time is one of providing a fair and objective listening ear and a place of security and love. A compassionate grandparent who is willing to let the child talk performs a necessary function. Wise grandparents are careful not to take sides, even on the side of their own child against the other parent.

ॐ

When they have been victimized by divorce, grandchildren are confused and hurt and often filled with anger, resentment, and guilt that they really don't understand. The role of the grandparent at this time is one of providing a fair and objective listening ear and a place of security and love.

We must listen and try to be objective, to help them understand that these adult problems are considerably beyond them. The incompatibilities of parents—sexual ones for instance—are totally incomprehensible to a preadolescent child. They don't understand enough about the entire sexual process to even know what it's all about. The child may have been used as a kind of ping-pong ball during the years prior to the divorce as the parents fought for the child's allegiance and attempted, in moments of despair and anger, to convince the child of the rightness or wrongness of each other's behavior.

By being a stable, unmovable, and fair listener, a grandparent can perform an invaluable service to the child. We become interpreters, helping the small child understand adult behavior. Helping the child to cope with this confusion is often the most important thing that a grandparent can do.

In addition to interpreting, we can also provide a climate in which healing can take place. Sometimes more talking only leads to a kind of wallowing in the problem. Sometimes it's time to quit talking, change the subject, and get on with life. We must do something besides constantly rehashing the situation. The grandparents' home can be the kind of place where children can play, have other interests, become involved in other conversations. It can be where they are allowed to just be without having to be loyal to or take sides with or be against one or the other parent.

Creating this climate of healing can be a gift to grandchildren that no amount of counseling or therapy could replace. The invitation, "You are welcome to come and stay with me for awhile," has saved many kids from ruin. As time passes, the ground shifts and parents reconcile or divorce, children get some rest and relief and new possibilities sometimes emerge. Kids with no place to go agonize in the midst of the storm and often drown in their parents' problems.

There is a natural tendency on the part of wounded teenagers to blame God for their pain. Theological reasoning by a pastor or grandparent can be of some limited value, but these feelings are often not really intellectual struggles over God's justice even though they may be stated that way. They are more often feelings of disappointment, loss, helplessness, and repressed anger. Living with grandparents and observing their steadfast faith is a more convincing argument than theology. Faith in the midst of the enormity of pain and loss has made the book of Job timeless.

We provide no real protection for children when we hold them tightly during a thunderstorm. But it would be impossible to convince the child of this—nor would we want to. What we can do is provide what we do have, a little more experience, a bit more courage and quiet, believing faith.

DEALING WITH GUILT

Another common problem that all children of divorce face is guilt. They've been told to be good and to behave, to keep certain rules. Like all human beings, they have failed. No child has yet been perfect or ever perfectly carried out the will of a parent. Sometimes they feel that the parents have broken up as a result of the problems they have brought to the family through disobedience. Though it would surprise many adults, most children of divorce feel that they contributed to or were responsible for their folks breaking up.

Usually the children did nothing, good or bad, to contribute to the divorce. Their parents are two adults with adult problems that they found were unsolvable. The child becomes the in-between person whose name comes up from time to time, but who has really had no active, causal relationship to the divorce. Grandparents can help to interpret the adult behavior, to assuage the children's guilt, to help them understand that they are victims of other people's actions, that they are just fine. Most likely, their parents would have broken up even if children had not been there. Youngsters need to be reassured that they had nothing to do with it and that they are helpless to solve the problem. They need to understand that no amount of "acting out" will help, even if they desperately want to hurt someone. They usually only hurt themselves.

A grandmother told me of her frustration with her granddaughter's promiscuous sexual behavior. Her daughter had been involved with multiple lovers and eventually had settled down with a man—not the father of her granddaughter but a man her daughter loved dearly. The man began to show inordinate interest in the child, which resulted in accusations toward the granddaughter of being a flirt.

Irresponsible things were said, and eventually the marriage broke up and the granddaughter was left to be raised by her grandmother. The girl felt totally worthless and was attempting to destroy herself with irresponsible sex—"If that's the kind of girl they think I am, then that's the kind of girl I'm going to be."

The grandmother said, "I just keep loving her and assuring her that this problem started long before she was born and that she does not have to punish herself for the breakup of her mother's marriage." This is the only winning approach for this grandmother to take, even though it is painful and she may feel as if she has betrayed her daughter. At some point we have to step in and try to break the ongoing pattern of behavior.

BREAKING THE CYCLE

Closely associated to guilt is another problem that most of these children face—feeling that there is a self-fulfilling prophecy at work in their lives: "If Mom and Dad divorced, then I will probably divorce, too." They've heard the statistics, that alcoholic parents produce alcoholic children, child abusers produce child abusers. They see divorce as a virus that has entered the family, and they are afraid of having any kind of stable relationships. They are afraid to trust and put their feet down, afraid to make commitments, because Mom and Dad divorced and they feel their marriages will end in divorce also. Statistically speaking, divorce does tend to be a self-perpetuating cycle; in individual cases, it need not be so.

Helping young people escape this cycle is an important role for grandparents. We must help them see that they can be different from their parents. We can help them see where their parents didn't handle things as well as they could have, and how they can start handling their problems differently. In many cases children of divorced parents have watched their parents' behavior and are unconsciously imitative of them. Oftentimes children whose parents lie and hedge and fudge on the truth find themselves doing the same thing. When children have watched their parents take shortcuts, they may also try to avoid consequences and not live honestly with cause and effect. People who rationalize their behavior tend to produce children who do the same.

Grandparents can exert a powerful influence by breaking through the cycle and helping grandchildren to see that if this kind of behavior is left unadjusted, they will end up being like their parents. "Yes, you are your dad's son," we can tell our grandchildren, "not because this is in your genetic makeup or because you're predestined to be this way, but because you're imitating the very behavior that has hurt you."

To help our grandchildren understand this while still maintaining respect for the parent and the parent's place of love, authority, and esteem in their eyes is no small task. We must help them redirect their anger away from the persons and toward the negative and destructive behavior.

I've found that biblical terminology is very helpful at this point. The concept of being "born again" carries the powerful image of a clean start. Being "new creatures," "all things becoming new," and "old things passing away" are hopeful ideas for kids caught in what feels like an impossible trap. A grandparent taking the time to look up helpful Bible verses and sharing them can be a tremendous support. There is power in God's Word.

Sometimes we may wish that human beings were like machines that could be adjusted with a wrench—one turn this direction, just this slight tension adjustment, and suddenly our problems are solved. But people are not machines. Parenting and grandparenting is more of an art than a science.

If you have a two-pound test line on your casting rod and you've hooked an eight-pound bass, it is a foregone conclusion that you cannot horse him into the boat by cranking on the reel. You will have to play him very, very carefully in order to save your line and land the fish. Some people never learn to do this, but for good fishermen, this is the skill they practice. They want to learn to land the fish with the right line, with a sense of sportsmanship.

Many parents may be too impatient and may break the line with their children, but the grandparent has had more experience. He or she knows how to use some finesse to accomplish the purpose with greater patience, wisdom, and greater insight.

ॐ

Young people dealing with the emotions of divorce desperately need around them people who are not caught up in the problem, who have not lost their objectivity, who are not totally partisan—people who can help them work through their sense of loss, their loneliness, their anger and confusion, their frustrations, and their guilt.

Almost without exception, young people tell me that they prefer to share their problems with grandparents. And grandparents feel they do better with grandchildren than they did with their children. I believe it truly has something to do with patience and confidence born of our experience, which assures us that we probably will survive the crisis. "This too shall pass" is a powerful principle only for someone who has seen some water pass under the bridge.

Young people dealing with the emotions of divorce desperately need around them people who are not caught up in the problem, who have not lost their objectivity, who are not totally partisan—people who can help them work through their sense of loss, their loneliness, their anger and confusion, their frustrations, and their guilt.

FORGETTING WHAT IS BEHIND...

Another universal problem that can be addressed by grandparents is the fact that both divorced parents and children of divorce often tend to see every human problem through the eyes of divorce. A divorced mother with a teenage son explains the boy's adolescent problems and says, "I'm sure it's because he doesn't have a father and I'm raising him alone."

But the problem has nothing to do with the fact that he doesn't have a father and she is raising him alone. Her husband might be a good listening ear if he were around, and he might provide some insight, but this is an adolescent problem, the kind of problem all teenage boys have. It has nothing to do with the divorce. It has to do with his age.

Solving the problem would probably be easier—or seem so—if two were working on it. But boys with fathers present have the same needs. Some problems are the direct result of the divorce and cannot be denied. It is a mistake, however, to give all of them this distinction. We must put our energy into solutions.

Similarly, children of divorce almost always preface their comments to me with, "My mom and dad got divorced; therefore, I am lonely." "My mom and dad are divorced; therefore, I am confused about my dating life." I attempt to help them to see that these are not problems due to divorce. They may not be able to talk to both parents about their problems, but many kids who are in very stable homes don't feel comfortable or free to discuss their problems with their parents.

I try to reassure them, "Your problem is you are human, you're an adolescent. These problems are normal, and you're okay to have these kinds of problems. Everyone does. Let's talk about the problem and how to solve it and get past this business of divorce."

Divorce, certainly, leaves deep scars and often has long-lasting effects. But the situation is often exacerbated by dwelling on the problem. People can die after a perfect diagnosis. Diagnosis has value only when it leads to a cure.

The Apostle Paul encourages us to "[forget] what is behind and [strain] toward what is ahead" (Phil 3:13). Paul probably would not oppose understanding root causes, but he stressed living life through the windshield rather than the rearview mirror.

Paul also stressed alternate activity and focus when he said, "Whatever is true, whatever is noble, whatever is right, whatever is pure... think about such things." Few people heal until they decide to move on from the problem toward new life. At one time or another in their lives, most grandparents have had to move on or sink. Our very survival is evidence to young people that survival is possible.

Few people heal until they decide to move on from the problem toward new life. Our very survival is evidence to young people that survival is possible.

We must strive for a sense of normalcy, facing the real problem rather than allowing it to remain in the "victim" category. We must try to help our grandchildren understand that while divorce is real and yes, it hurts; while it's always there and will never be otherwise, this is a problem we can solve. Grandparents must try to convince their grandchildren that we are here and available and plan to see them through. We may not have dealt with this specific problem, but we have been through some deep waters. We can tell them, "This too will pass, even though at this point it is hard to see how. One thing we do know is that we will do it together." This is, incidentally, the same promise God makes to us—not that he will remove or solve all of our problems, but "I will never leave you or forsake you!"

When divorced adult children live in the house belonging to their parents, they naturally feel impotent, unable to cope. They feel as if they're not adult; they have failed. As parents of divorced children, we can repeat, "This is working out all right; it isn't a problem; you're not in the way." But still, grown children who are forced to take charity from their own parents feel demeaned and will often react in bizarre and unpredictable ways. Their loss of self-esteem may cause them to engage in withdrawal, in acts of self-denigration, or sometimes even in hostility. They may lash out in anger against the situation, not realizing that they have picked the wrong target. We always hurt the ones we love because they are close to us.

Grandparents can be caught in the middle trying to do the right thing, to be loving and charitable. We often may need to spend a good deal of time in prayer, coming to terms with understanding our divorced children, forgiving them their outbursts and irresponsible behavior. We must realize that there is a much larger principle at stake here and attempt to provide an environment in which our grandchildren can grow into normalcy and somehow escape the ravages that divorce breeds.

FIELDING RESPONSIBILITY

One of the toughest aspects of grandparenting the children of divorce is the energy factor. Children were designed for younger parents, and at the age when most people become grandparents, we are not temperamentally suited for raising children and solving the problems parenting entails. We must depend upon God if we want to be up to the task.

Almost everyone can bear a headache or a toothache if they know it will end soon. We can all turn our heads and get a shot or have a doctor perform a painful procedure for a few seconds. But realizing that we may be stuck with this problem for the next twenty years is quite another thing. All the years we planned to spend in retirement are going to be taken up with raising grandchildren and solving grown children's problems. We can give in to despair, fear, and anger, usually expressed toward the divorced parent.

When grandchildren overhear or observe tension between parent and grandparent, they feel responsible for the situation. They think that perhaps if they weren't in the grandparents' household then Grandma and Grandpa wouldn't be upset, they wouldn't be picking on Mom or Dad. The young person may attempt to run away or try to do something for attention—drugs, alcohol, suicide. Kids considering suicide have often said to me, "Now maybe everyone will know how sorry I am." They sincerely feel they are a problem for everyone, and the world would be better off if they weren't around. They often reach out for assurance through acts of self-punishment.

Sharing our feelings openly and admitting the tension is much preferable to a smoldering, festering resentment-filled environment. For Christians, praying together, confessing our confusion, and seeking God's presence can be a bonus not understood by secular people.

Grandchildren who have been abandoned face an even greater problem. It is easier for a young grandchild to understand the death of a parent than the abandonment of a parent. When Dad is killed in a war or an automobile accident or dies of a heart attack, when Mother has died in childbirth or succumbed to cancer, young children feel sad, lonely, angry at God, and short-changed by life. But because there is something final about it they are able to handle it.

But when a parent abandons a child and simply says, "I don't care about you"—either overtly or by implication, leaving without accepting responsibility—the grandparent faces a deep problem. In one way or another the grandparent ends up needing to say that indeed the parent is irresponsible. "Yes, your mother is self-absorbed. We just have to admit that she has her own set of problems. She has lost herself in alcohol or drugs; she prefers to run around with other men and neglect you. That is true. We hope she'll grow up. She's my daughter. I love her and always will. But in the meantime you must understand that you are not responsible for this, and you are loved. We love you supremely and won't let you fall. We're here for you."

As we seek to reach out to abandoned grandchildren, we can tell them the family stories of people who've been kept by aunts and uncles and loved by grandparents so they don't feel as if they're alone. We can give them something stable under their feet. We might not prefer these situations, but we can make the best of them.

Some of the most stable young people I've encountered

in my life have been raised by grandparents. Even now at Taylor University, students bring their grandma and grandpa to meet me—grandparents who have raised them. I always feel a great sense of pride in these grandparents. Each family has its own story.

Leo Tolstoy began his novel *Anna Karenina* with a very interesting statement: "All happy families are alike, but all unhappy families are unhappy in their own way." Each of these unhappy families has a story, but there are some heroic stories in them as well. Often it falls to the grandparents to provide the happy ending to these stories.

In the Old Testament story of Joseph, God made work out for good what was intended by his brothers for evil. It is a long story with many twists and turns, but in the end Joseph's faith and perseverance win out.

❧

When divorce does happen, the grandparents can become the stabilizing influence to make a lasting difference between tragedy and redemption.

Even though we've learned to accept divorce in our society, no one is really an advocate of divorce. Divorced people don't think it's the best solution to their problems—it's just the only one available at the time, given the circumstances as they perceive them. When it does happen, the grandparents can become the stabilizing influence to make a lasting difference between tragedy and redemption.

Parenting a five-year-old when you're sixty is no simple task, but it can be done. Trying to counsel a teenage granddaughter about her love life and dating may test the mind of the grandfather, but with some effort he may remember when he felt that same way. With patience and understanding, he can be the listening ear that she desperately needs.

A friend of mine was pastor of a large inner-city church. He had carried the responsibilities for many years and was exhausted in every way. He felt spiritually empty and emotionally drained. But he was embarrassed to admit this to his staff or fellow pastors because, after all, he was supposed to be the leader.

In desperation he sought out an elderly nun he had met at a conference and, confident that she did not know any of his friends or parishioners, spilled out his soul. She listened patiently and then said, "Try as hard as you can to describe your true feelings, not just the circumstances."

He thought deeply and then said, "I feel like an old farm pump that has been pumped dry. Everybody wants water and they are all pumping my handle, but I'm just bringing up air. It's like I have the dry heaves."

She said, "I think I have the picture. Why don't you come back tomorrow and after I've prayed about it, I'll give a response." They held hands and prayed, and he left.

The next day he visited her office and she said, "I need to clarify one thing. Did you enter the ministry because you wanted to be used of God?"

"Oh, yes!" he replied, "that's the whole point of my life."

"Then the problem isn't that you don't want to be a pump, and certainly the people aren't wrong for wanting water," she said. "What you need to do is get your pipe down deeper so it's in the water." Together they entered into a covenant of prayer and spiritual discipline and he was not only able to cope, but entered a new level of spiritual insight.

ॐ

If we get our pipes down deep into God's water, we can do far beyond what we could imagine in our own strength.

Most grandparents caught in the responsibility of raising grandchildren tell me later that what amazes them most is how well it works, not how poorly it works. They are quite astonished that the friends of their grandchildren tend to seek them out and enjoy being around them. This baffles many grandparents carrying out the role of parent, but I believe that God gives them what they need to fulfill his purposes for their lives.

When the demands of our lives are overwhelming, God's grace is greater. If we get our pipes down deep into God's water, we can do far beyond what we could imagine doing in our own strength.

TEN

When In-Laws Become Out-Laws

I F I HAD DIED before I had the chance to become a grand-parent, I might have felt a little gypped. When it first happened, of course, I was sure it couldn't possibly happen to someone as young and virile as myself. *How could my daughter possibly be old enough to be married to this man and produce a child?* I thought. And I was totally unprepared for the emotions that took place when she had the real live baby. Being a grandparent was no longer an idea, it was a reality with all kinds of new emotions and relationships.

But within the first few minutes after I had seen the new grandchild and felt so special, I realized I was not the only grandfather on the block. There was another set of grandparents who felt every bit as close, as honored, and as important and primary as we did.

Thus begins an interesting dynamic, closely akin to what we face when our children marry and we discover that we must share them with in-laws for holidays and family celebrations. Occasionally they are unable to be at our house because they are at the "other" family's home, and we have to mature past our petty resentments and selfish whims. We must realize that this is part of the scheme of things as we blend our families and provide support for our children.

In the same way, with our grandchildren, we must also realize that fair is fair. They *will* be spending time with the other grandparents.

And sometimes the other grandparents are more fun than we are. They may have more money than we do. Their house may look like an amusement park. They may have resources at their disposal—ponies, boats, country clubs, swimming pools—that we don't have. Or we may have those things, to their chagrin.

૨૦

> *The grandchildren dare not be put in competition to decide who the favorite grandparent is.*

Either way, we must deal with the reality that the grandchildren dare not be put in competition to decide who the favorite grandparent is.

I think it's important that rules be set up in the beginning. We should always be supportive of the other grandparents and speak well of them, never with criticism. This is a winning formula, not just a polite one. If you try to do otherwise, the children will sense it and find it difficult to be open with you in sharing their experiences. They may become defensive or they may try to work us against each other for their own gain.

When we've heard that they've been at the other grandparents' house we need to find out how things have gone and to participate in their joy and excitement rather than looking crestfallen. This takes a bit of maturity, but maturity is what we have to offer as grandparents. If we can't offer maturity, all we have to offer is old age—and getting old is not the same as being mature. Maturity produces graciousness, patience, wisdom, and other virtues.

એ

If we can't offer maturity, all we have to offer is old age—and getting old is not the same as being mature.

SHOWDOWN WITH THE OUT-LAWS

When my son Bruce was about twelve years old, I received a call from a good friend saying, "Say, Jay, how about taking our sons on a canoe trip on Saturday?" He had a boy about five years old, so we were going to take two canoes, two dads, and two boys and go down the river. We would take both cars, put my car at the end of the run, and take his car twenty miles upstream with the canoes.

I arrived with my son on the appointed day at the appointed place, and to my surprise, there were *three* canoes on top of his car carrier and *four* people standing by the car—his son, himself, and two older men. My son and I got out and shook hands and discovered the two older men were the two grandfathers—my friend's father and his father-in-law. One of the grandfathers, who was a little obnoxious, acted as if he knew a lot about everything. He proceeded to tell us how to get the canoes off the roof and place them in the river.

I didn't bother to tell him that I earned my living in youth work and youth camping and had more experience with canoes than most North American Indians. Because I was his junior, I allowed him to tell me all these details and tried to appear interested. My son, knowing my experience with canoeing, got a kick out of listening to the elderly man order me around.

We got the canoes in the river and then the question arose, "Who will canoe with the grandson?" They decided to flip a coin to determine who would canoe with whom. My son and I got in our canoe and they flipped a coin. The quieter grandfather won the toss and got the grandson in his canoe. The father and the loud grandfather got in the other canoe.

We decided to allow them to go first down the river so we could pick up the strays and if anything happened we could be of help since we were more experienced. As we started downstream, we had only gone half a mile when the grandfather and grandson tipped the canoe over. The little fellow went into the water. It wasn't really deep and not too dangerous, and I had no concern for the little guy's well-being. He was equipped with a life jacket, but the water was very cold, so when his head went under water, he began to cry and was quite frightened. We got out and helped him, but he was still terrified.

The loud-mouthed grandfather began to give advice as to why the canoe had tipped in the first place, and explained what the other grandfather had done wrong. The poor timid grandfather was crestfallen and disappointed. His grandson had gotten wet at his expense, and he felt extremely bad. He tried to console the little boy, but the boy wouldn't allow himself to be comforted—after all, Grandpa had allowed him to fall out of the canoe and get his head wet.

The "know-it-all" grandfather insisted the boy go with him. We placed him in that canoe and returned to ours. When we had enough distance between us that no one could overhear, my son said, "Boy, I really feel sorry for his granddad. He's such a nice man, and the little boy is treating him bad." Half a mile further downstream, the canoe tipped over again, and the little boy got wet a second time. He was crying and about to decide that he despised them all—canoes, water, rivers, *and* grandpas.

The quiet grandfather resisted smiling and said nothing, although he might have had the right to look at heaven, hold both hands in the air and proclaim, "There is a God after all!"

The little boy could not be consoled. He wouldn't allow either grandfather to touch him. He didn't want to get drowned by either one any more.

We ended the last eighteen miles of the trip with the two grandfathers in one canoe, not talking to each other, just sullenly paddling. My son and I were in one canoe and my friend and his son in the other, enjoying eighteen miles of good river canoeing and the sense of well-being you get when you see living proof of the justice of God.

This experience taught me that it's foolish to view my grandchildren as a symbol of my own importance; it's foolish to be competitive over them. Neither grandfather was at fault; canoes flip over. If you don't want to flip over in the water, walk on dry land. If you don't want to have any excitement, spend your whole life in the family room.

The child didn't know any better, but grandfathers should be mature enough to handle these situations without losing their temper or their cool, and especially without using a grandchild as a pawn.

We can all learn an important lesson about dealing with the feelings of jealousy and competition that turn the in-laws into out-laws. We need confidence in ourselves, we need to be secure enough to realize that though we may not be like the other set of grandparents, we still have something to offer. Our house has its own charm, our way of life has its own value, we don't have to compare it with theirs or try to outdo them. There is no need for one-upmanship. We don't need to buy the most expensive gifts, spend the most money, and lavish the grandchildren with all of our attention. Just being ourselves and being true to our own values will hold us in good stead over the long run.

Over time, the in-laws can become friends, and at some point both sets of grandparents may be called upon to provide the support grandchildren need.

SPIRITUAL INCOMPATIBILITY

Many of the tensions of in-law relationships can be handled in a routine manner, even though they sometimes take on the comic proportions of our canoe trip. But other situations are more complex and are not resolved so easily. A number of these problems have to do with spiritual incompatibility and the conflicting influences that result.

Lifestyles. One concerned grandmother said, "We're not a rigid family, but I do resent the fact that when our grandchildren visit their other grandparents they get away with doing mean things to each other. Because everyone swears, they do too, and no one seems concerned. In fact, they say, 'That's the way boys are; we don't want them to be sissies.' They also drink and smoke, and although the kids don't do that, I think it's a bad example. What should we do?"

In such case concern is justified, but to take the wrong approach might make matters worse. To begin with we should work to make our Christian homes more creative, more exciting, more accepting than non-Christian homes. Otherwise kids associate stiffness, taking ourselves too seriously, and being a spoil-sport with the gospel. Most Christian homes are already portrayed this way in movies or sit-coms. The effort that we put forth to make our homes attractive not only encourages our grandchildren to like us, but also to like God. It is one thing for a young person to have to deal with media stereotypes, but quite another if the stereotype is the truth. Joy is one of the fruits of the Spirit and should be a natural part of a Christian home.

When grandchildren ask about such activities as smoking, swearing, and drinking, it is important that we do not speak in a derogatory or condescending way lest grandchildren feel the need to be defensive of the other grandparents. Kids will almost always take the side of anyone they feel is being picked on. It is best, as the old song says, to "accentuate the positive" or to avoid commenting at all. If our grandchildren press the issue, we can explain that different people live in different ways and we choose not to do these things.

It is probably best not to add the phrase, "because we are Christians and they are not." First of all, that makes us sound as if we feel superior. Second, it is simply not true; it *is* possible to be a Christian and still do these things. We are saved through grace, not because we don't smoke, drink, or swear. We must seek to live out the fruit of the Spirit so convincingly that the kids will prefer our lifestyle.

If our Christian walk is consistent and the other set of grandparents ridicule us, the same sense of justice that causes kids to try to protect the underdog will work to our benefit. In the meantime, we can pray for both the grandchildren and their grandparents, trusting that the Holy Spirit can accomplish what we find impossible.

Indulgence. Often grandparents write and say, "The other grandparents are ruining our grandchildren with gifts. They indulge them in every way, and I'm afraid they will grow up spoiled and unable to function without having everything handed to them on a silver platter. We feel that they should learn to work and appreciate what they have."

It is very hard to convince children—or, for that matter, most adults—that doing without is more fun than having everything you desire. We simply must be patient and wait for them to experience the emptiness that indulgence always produces. In the short term it is very difficult to watch. We must bank on the strength of sincere love, personal availability, an empathetic heart, patience, and the power of prayer linked with example. It is also wise not to overdo it for the sake of principle. Reasonable and thoughtful gifts, including those that are fun, are not a vice. We struggle against overindulgence, not generosity.

Acceptance. When we are dealing with in-law grandparents, a general rule about intervention certainly applies: it is never wise or even effective to confront, criticize, or make suggestions if we are unable or unprepared to be involved in the process of helping the person overcome the problem. When intervention is necessary, there is always a price to pay.

I saw a dramatic example of such intervention recently. A family who hosted me in their home for a weekend were the grandparents of two preschool children. The other grandmother was an alcoholic and nearly nonfunctional. Though she was very nearly the age of my hosts, she seemed old and unsure of herself. She was a kind and shy person who seemed to suffer from a deep sense of unworthiness and guilt. My hosts included her in their weekend activities, helped her navigate the task of getting into the car and ordering her food in the restaurant. They invited her to spend the afternoon with the family and treated her with respect. I'm not sure how much of the situation the grandchildren understood, but I could see that the grandparents approached the incompatibility with creativity, grit, and Christian grace.

&

It is never wise or even effective to confront, criticize, or make suggestions if we are unable or unprepared to be involved in the process of helping the person overcome the problem.

Whether we like them or not, we are connected with the "out-law" grandparents; our grandchildren are the coupling between us. If the "other grandparents" are Christians, we may forge a family connection based on that common bond. If they are not, we might, through our love and acceptance, offer them an attractive picture of the God we serve. In either case, the less strain we put on this connection, the better off our grandchildren will be.

ELEVEN

Surrogate Grandparents

ONCE UPON A TIME in American history, most families lived in small clusters—either in villages or towns, or in ethnic neighborhoods in great cities. Young people almost universally had the opportunity of living near their cousins, their aunts and uncles, but most importantly, their grandparents. Divorce was virtually unknown and families had much greater continuity.

Today we are surrounded by families that have experienced divorce, abandonment, alcoholism, or death; they have been blended two or three times in an attempt to find stability and a place of family love, growth and nurture.

FINDING THE MISSION FIELD

The incidence of single parents is quite high in our churches, and even higher across the broader culture. If we truly want to minister to those children who are torn apart by broken homes, we can begin to do something about it. We do not need to spend money or travel overseas to find our mission field. It is all around us—in our neighborhood, in our apartment building, in our church. We can take the role of surrogate grandparents.

🐝

Our mission field is all around us—in our neighborhood, in our apartment building, in our church.

As our children were growing up, we lived about two-and-a-half hours from their grandparents. We made every effort to be together on holidays, and we worked hard making certain our children had meaningful contacts with their grandparents. Thankfully, they have fond memories and have been profoundly affected by them.

My father has left a lasting impression on his grandchildren from the standpoint of Christian social concern. He was obsessed with poverty and racial injustice. He spoke of this so often in their presence, and with such conviction and eloquence, that all of them have carried a sense of Christian social responsibility into their definitions of the gospel. They evaluate political candidates not only in economic terms but in moral and ethical ways, especially in terms of compassion for the poor. Our son Bruce has devoted his life to working with inner-city, disadvantaged youth.

The grandparent gap. But even though we spent as much time as possible with the grandparents, because we lived far from them there was still a gap. An older couple in our church filled this need—our children called them Grandpa and Grandma Terhune. The Terhunes invited our kids over for meals by themselves. They took them places. As our children grew older, they helped the Terhunes mow their lawn. Grandma and Grandpa Terhune involved our children in their activities, and the kids experienced from this couple a great deal of what they would have received from their own grandparents had they been nearer.

I was a little surprised that our kids chose the Terhunes as surrogate grandparents. Mrs. Terhune was a stereotypical grandma from a storybook, but her husband Max was a bit of a grouch. We became close friends, yet he could be exasperating, as old men are expected to be. Max always told it as he saw it—not necessarily as everybody should see it, but as *he* saw it. It's probably the same quality Herod saw in John the Baptist that made him tolerate the prophet for so long.

Examples of faith. Our son Bruce overheard many of my conversations with Max. He knew that Max had deep faith, even though life had been less than easy for him. On the occasion of his sixtieth wedding anniversary I congratulated him and said, "Wow, Max! Sixty years is a long time—you may have the record in our church."

"Not bad," he replied, "considering she was my second wife!"

Max had married in his early twenties and lost his first wife to influenza after about a year and a half. This second marriage had produced several children, one who was mildly retarded and one who was afflicted with polio and endured lifelong impairment in walking. Bruce heard him say to me many times, "Jay, what we need to realize is that life is real." To him, "life is real" meant that you go on, you persevere, you do not question God. You live by faith and rise above it. To him it was a sin to complain. "Life is real" means that the Christian life must be lived out in the midst of difficult circumstances.

Bruce heard all of this and for his own reasons decided to love Max and adopt him as a surrogate grandfather whether he liked it or not. Max did like it, and we were grateful for the Terhunes' influence as we were trying to hold on to family values in the midst of Chicago's suburban sprawl. Our kids had grandparents, yet distance made it difficult to bridge the intergenerational gap without a boost from someone else.

愛

I strongly urge mature Christians to look around the congregation and ask God to lay certain children on your heart. Search for those natural affinities and connections and begin the process of bringing these children under your wing.

There are thousands of young people who need the advantage of surrogate grandparents in a much more desperate sense. Many children have never been around older people; they know nothing of the generations. They live as "cut flowers" and have few if any roots. They desperately need contact with caring, Christian grandparents. I strongly urge mature Christians to look around the congregation and ask God to lay certain children on your heart. Search for those natural affinities and connections and begin the process of bringing these children under your wing.

LOSING YOUR LIFE TO FIND IT

The Terhunes were not the only couple in our church who served as surrogate grandparents. Ed and Lil Meyer, whose children had left home many years before, performed an important function for our entire church. For nearly twenty years, every child in church had a very sharp memory of Halloween, when Lil would take down her gray hair that reached almost to the floor, comb it out, powder it to make it even grayer, and sit in her rocking chair in a long dress on the porch, waiting for children to come by for Trick or Treat. This funny, slightly frightening character stuck in the minds of all children.

Their parents would cajole them up the porch steps, past Lil as she sat in her chair. Then she would reach out and grab them and welcome them to her house, where Ed was waiting with his ever-present bags of candies. Along with the treats, they gave out warm memories that old people are good and nice, not people to be afraid of or ignored as if they don't exist. Because they were interested in kids and because they knew how to have fun, all the kids called them Grandma Lil and Grandpa Ed.

ટે&

Grandparents can "lose their lives"
for young people and make a
profound difference.

At Christmas time Ed and Lil would exhaust themselves putting out their Christmas decorations. Over a period of years, Ed had collected a Christmas village made up of hundreds of little houses, trains, cars, people, and churches. It covered some ten square feet on the living room floor and flowed up onto the tables around the house. A child coming to Ed's and Lil's house at Christmas could sit for hours and simply be fascinated by these little scenes—the snowflakes, horses, sleighs, and reindeer—the memories of Christmas. Ed and Lil did this as a gesture of love, as substitute grandparents caring about children and their joy at Christmas time. Grandparents don't need to sit home and vegetate, complaining about growing health problems. They can "lose their lives" for young people and make a profound difference.

Another grandfather has spent virtually every weekend of the summer for the last several years, pulling his grandsons and their friends around his little lake on their water skis. He's burned up more gasoline than he would like to admit and has doubtless spent more money on repairs to his boat than he can keep track of. Yet as a grandfather, he has communicated through these many hours the care and love and concern that he has for his grandchildren. He has also transmitted to them his basic value system.

I have watched the kids take the cover off the boat and prepare it for use. After they are finished, they put the cover back on, wipe it down, and do the maintenance tasks. As I watch, I believe these boys will be better citizens, better employees, better parents, better contributors to the world because of this regular contact with their grandpa, who has been willing to spread himself out and let their friends in on this family experience. These boys and their endless string of friends are experiencing grandfathering in a modern setting.

WHAT'S REALLY IMPORTANT

Recently Paul Newman and Joanne Woodward were honored by a tribute at the John F. Kennedy Center for the Performing Arts. A film presentation highlighted their acting and directing careers, showing portions of *Hud, Cool Hand Luke, Mr. and Mrs. Bridge* and a host of other films.

The commendation then shifted to a camp that they had donated for children with terminal illnesses, named "Camp Hole in the Wall," after the gang in *Butch Cassidy and the Sundance Kid*. A group of these children came on stage and thanked the Newmans and then sang a song for their benefit. Both of them lost their composure and wiped tears from their eyes. Obviously this part of their lives brought more satisfaction than all of their movies combined. Being surrogate grandparents to these children and supplementing the care of their parents provided untold joy.

Few of us have the fame or visibility of Paul Newman and Joanne Woodward; few of us have enough money to adopt several dozen children as surrogates. But all who care, rich and poor, can find some place of contributing to the world's grandchildren.

As grandparents, we can read the newspaper, listen to the news—and spend all of our time wringing our hands about the breakdown of the American family. Or, rather than cursing the darkness, we can light our own candle and open our lives to those around us, allowing young people to see us as surrogates.

Surrogate grandparenting can be done in any neighborhood, and indeed, has been done by grandparents for many generations. Within the church, however, it is possible to do it in a more meaningful and intimate way. We can fill a gap for people who are extremely isolated, who find themselves cut off from their own families. In every church there are single parents, struggling in an attempt to make ends meet and be responsible. Grandparents can be surrogates to these people, having them over for Sunday meals so they can experience the friendship, support, and strength that God intended for families.

èa

Rather than cursing the darkness, we can light our own candle and open our lives to those around us, allowing young people to see us as surrogates.

Even in the college setting, young people from relatively stable homes need this kind of reinforcement. On the Taylor campus, we have several couples who open their homes virtually any time young people are willing to come. These are people whose children have grown and left home a long time ago. They are willing to hear and understand, to listen, to provide a place for young people to test their ideas, share their dreams, and sometimes do a little raving about the problems they face, both real and imagined. These are places where they can relax and entrust their thoughts to an older person who cares enough to listen and give them the advantage of their experiences. These surrogates are invited to weddings, visited during the summer, and included in Christmas card lists. They have babies named after them and are mourned sincerely, all because they were available and opened their homes.

THE FOUNTAIN OF YOUTH

Carrie Thompson, who celebrated her ninetieth birthday last year has spent her life as an executive secretary.

She has held many responsible jobs, and now as she has grown older, she seeks to be a surrogate grandparent, volunteering to help in different ministries. She works at the local camp for underprivileged children stuffing mail, helping them to prepare their monthly newsletter. They all call her Grandma. She volunteers at the local school as a kindergarten teacher's assistant, and even at her age, actually sits on the floor and at the little tables, helping the children with their handwork. I wonder if she does this because she's in such good health, or if she is in such good health because she does these things.

Interestingly, she rather resents being thought of as grandmotherly. "I do what I do," she says. "It doesn't matter how old I am." Such insistence on being useful is part of her charm.

I have seen the same kind of attitude in my own mother. I have taken courses in urban sociology and psychology of the adolescent, and have attended seminars on drug-related problems, the problems of the inner city, and racial tensions. But while I have been attending courses and urban conferences so I could equip and challenge the church to a response, my mother has simply gone into the inner city each week to teach a group of young blacks in a nearly abandoned downtown church. She helps these kids with Bible lessons and their memory verses, bakes them cookies, and gets to know them by name. They surround her and listen as she shares her faith with them and she listens to their concerns. They call her Grandma Kesler, and she knows each of them by name. They see her as an extension of whatever families they have. Her weekly visit into their neighborhood brings a sense of predictability, a strength they wouldn't have in situations that are often confusing and undependable.

Over the years I have met people who seem to have lifted themselves by their own bootstraps out of terrible brokenness. Almost without exception they point to a caring adult, a surrogate parent or grandparent who made all the difference. At the secular level, there are many illustrations of this. But Christian surrogates have at their disposal the power of the gospel itself, the Word of God, the prayers, and the work of the Holy Spirit to transform lives.

୧ଈ

*Christian surrogates have at their disposal
the power of the gospel itself, the
Word of God, the prayers, and the work
of the Holy Spirit to transform lives.*

A CUP OF COLD WATER

Such influence can happen across racial lines and cultural barriers. Shelby Steele, in his book *The Content of Our Character,* writes with tremendous clarity about the current American situation. In his book, Steele, a black man, recounts an experience with a white woman who befriended him at the YMCA and attempted to counsel him when he was a small boy. At first he resented it as coming from a white woman because he was preconditioned to suspect the motives of people like her.

Now in mid-life, as he looks back on the important friendships and interactions that molded his life, Steele gives a profound and insightful tribute to her contribution to his life. What may have seemed to her like a very small thing, befriending a small boy who was a friend of her son at the local YMCA, has become one of the anchor points in his understanding of human relationships. As a National Book Critic Circle Award winner and a *New York Times* best seller, Steele is able to share the power of her lesson with millions of readers. His message of self-reliance, hard work, honest accomplishment, and anti-racism is not accepted by all, yet he is a bright light in the midst of a bleak landscape. One small gesture by a caring elder contributed to this hopeful and positive example.

This is the power the gospel refers to when it speaks of giving a cup of cold water in Jesus' name. The power of the surrogate grandparent in our culture has not been fully addressed by the church, but I believe it needs to be and can be.

SHEPHERDS FOR THE SHEEP

A few months ago I was invited to do a series of lectures and sermons at a large urban church. One of the meetings scheduled was a session with the senior citizens in the church. This particular group was not willing to simply come to church, eat cookies, and drink coffee. They were discussing the ways they could maximize the time they had on their hands. In talking to them I told them of a man in my church who had grown very old. He said he had "long days, weary hours, and much time to pray."

The group went on to talk about what they can do before they reach a state where they can spend virtually full-time in prayer for those around them. We made a long list of activities. I was utterly amazed at the preoccupation of these people with the well-being of their grand-children and their vision for making a difference.

Without exception they talked about the young people running unaccompanied through the church. They re-membered when all the children were brought to church by their parents. Now so many of the children seemed unattended. This bothered them, not because of their noise or unruliness, but because they saw the children as sheep without a shepherd—the very image that Jesus saw when he looked at Jerusalem. Shepherds for the sheep... this is the role that grandparents can play as surrogates.

This year, Janie and I had agreed to go to the local junior high school to see the class project of a professor's son. The boy was the age of our grandchildren; we intended to support that one boy and show interest in his work.

When we arrived, we went from classroom to class-room, booth to booth, and discovered that we knew sev-eral of the children and their parents as well. These are children whose grandparents live in other parts of the country. As we walked from room to room looking at their projects on international culture, the kids clung to us and wanted to show us what they had done. Without intend-ing it, we found ourselves fulfilling the role of grand-parents.

Many of those children did not have grandparents who could attend the day's activities. Simply to have us walk-ing through the school, taking one hour of one day to applaud their hard work, made an enormous impact. They followed us and shared with us, chattering and talk-ing and telling us the stories behind their projects. Later we got cards from them, thanking us for stopping by and showing an interest in them.

FILLING UP THE VACUUM

The older generation is often highly critical of the younger one. Some people believe that there is an innate generation gap that separates us from one another, and yet I find that young people, who often seem so far away and so strange, often have a great thirst for a little interest shown by somebody.

Perhaps their fascination with MTV and video games may simply demonstrate that nature abhors a vacuum. Perhaps these people we criticize for being crassly commercial and preying on our youth are simply moving into areas left open to them by the preoccupation, fears, and selfishness of an adult generation who will not take the time to show interest in them.

As grandparents, we need to look up from the hymnal, to look around the church, to find young people to befriend. We can share a smile, ask a question, show interest in these children; and perhaps we can provide more than simply our tithes and offerings to the church of Jesus Christ in this modern and very needy age.

Not all children, of course, will respond to the overtures of surrogate grandparents, and not all single parents will welcome our presence. And we will no doubt have less in common with some than with others. But by the time we've reached grandparenting age, we should be familiar with the risk of rejection and able to deal with it. We need to try to open doors, to make overtures, to offer to be available. It is not usually complicated to determine who is really interested. As we are aware from other relationships, those in need often will show their need by hanging around, by seeking us out, by watching for us in the church foyer. Sometimes it does take courage and perseverance, and an overcoming spirit, but the risk of rejection is not a great price to pay for personal meaning and relevance.

Ed and Lil Meyer, surrogate grandparents to our own children, made a profound impact on our church. One of Ed's grandparenting contributions was passing out candy and gum to the children in the foyer before and after services. He did this without a great deal of forethought. Ed simply liked children and wanted them to like him and the church. It didn't go much deeper than that, but it provided joy for both Ed and the kids.

A flap developed when some young mothers who were concerned about candy's effect on their children's dental hygiene began to complain. Ed began to bring sugarless gum in an attempt to adjust to these concerns. But a couple of the women drew the line and refused to allow him to give anything to their children. Perhaps they were concerned about their children getting in the habit of taking candy from strangers. They asked me to tell him to quit passing out candy to the children in the church. I wanted to argue with them, but I realized that their concerns were legitimate.

A child with a cavity in his mouth is one thing; a child with a cavity in his heart is quite another. For Ed, the candy was simply an entry point, a symbol, a gesture to get acquainted. What he and Lil were and did for youth and the church was profound. They loved kids, noticed them, made them feel important and modeled Christian maturity.

I approached Ed and explained their concerns and asked him to not pass out candy any longer in the foyer. Tears actually ran down Ed's face as we talked. He understood, but he was deeply wounded because he had never thought of harming a child. He was attempting to fill a need in the lives of these suburban children, to be a grandfather to children whose own grandparents were far away.

The look on Ed's face was the same look that elementary teachers get when they are told they may no longer hug or touch their students in any circumstance, except to yank them out of harm's way. Ed actually spent a week or two in a kind of withdrawn state. Then I began to see him back in the church, befriending the children, handing them pens and other gifts that were acceptable to the children and parents as a gesture of love.

Over time some of these mothers came to understand the difference between concern for their children's teeth and the larger concern of a cultural void in their children's lives. We experience this void today as we live in isolation from one another. In a world marked by mass communication and cutting-edge technology, the human touch is the missing element.

êð

The roadsides today are filled with young people who need our love. As grandparents—actual or surrogate— we can take on the role of good Samaritan, binding wounds, giving of ourselves, and healing the hurts with love.

We certainly want good teeth, good diet, and professional teachers. We want to avoid the trauma of sexual abuse. We need, however, to be careful that we do not become so over-sensitized that we miss the small touches, the humanity that souls need to thrive and grow. In the greatest, most advanced society on the earth, many young people do not have the advantage of these fond memories that can provide stability, hope, and a role model for their future. It takes initiative and courage to make the gesture, and there may be some risks. But our family can attest to the value of Ed Meyer, Max Terhune, and Carrie Thompson being surrogate grandparents for our children.

If Jesus told the story of the good Samaritan within our culture, it might give us new insights about what one person can do to help another. The lawyer simply wanted to talk about the man in theory. The thieves preyed upon his vulnerability and weakness. The religious leaders avoided contact lest he interfere with their plans and schedules. The innkeeper did what he was paid to do. But the good Samaritan inconvenienced himself, overcame his fears, spent some of his own money, and showed him compassion. The roadsides today are filled with young people who need our love. As grandparents—actual or surrogate—we can take on the role of good Samaritan, binding wounds, giving of ourselves, and healing the hurts with love.

TWELVE

Meaning through Mortality

I HAVE OFTEN HEARD older adults say, "This is the greatest period of my life. If I didn't know what follows it, I would enjoy it a great deal more." We often engage in such slightly macabre humor after middle age, acknowledging a kind of subliminal preoccupation with our own mortality. We all know that we're eventually going to die. But dying is often preceded by years of physical struggle, and we resist admitting that we may have to endure ill health or struggle with maladies commonly associated with old age.

The reality of our lives stands in stark contrast to the society in which our grandchildren are living. Today's culture idolizes youth and good health almost as a cult. We see young people on television commercials exercising at expensive spas with complicated machines, dressed in leotards that reveal the kind of perfect bodies we can only imagine. A friend of mine said once, "I'm eighty-eight years old, and when I get out of the shower and stand in front of the mirror, I find it very humorous. I'm actually living in this wrinkled body! I feel mentally just as I did when I was twenty-one, but there I am zipped inside this old body and I can't escape it. I find it really kind of funny."

Today's world labors under a denial of old age, an almost universal resistance to a very important part of the cycle of life. Life is not simply birth, childhood, adolescence and sexual vitality. Part of the life cycle involves eventual maturation, old age, and death.

AGING GRACEFULLY

Virtually all of life's experiences are original, unique to us when we have them. I often tell parents that they can't get a plastic baby to practice on when they become parents. They get a real live child right out of the chute. From day one they have real problems, and they learn to cope with them based on vicarious observations of how their parents coped, the remembrance of their own youth, and certain helpful books and discussions that give advice on how it should be done.

The same is true of growing old. We've never done it before, never faced the kinds of problems that old age brings. How we cope with this new experience, however, can telegraph very important messages to those watching us, especially our grandchildren. Some people obviously hate it and it shows in all they do. Others seem to do it quite well. I'm convinced that how gracefully we grow older is basically a decision we make. Happiness is usually a choice, not a result.

Eastern cultures and religions are well known for their reverence for the aged, and sometimes we tend to relegate such respect to "outdated Oriental custom." But if we study the Scripture upon which Western civilization is built, we find that the Judeo-Christian tradition reverences and respects old age as well.

Something has happened to modern culture that seems to be going cross-current with our underpinnings and our past. It is easy these days to hide the unpleasant, to deny it, to put older people in special parts of the country, in special housing, by and large to carry on a busy life of youth, education, and commerce separate from older adults.

But as grandparents we are the only models of "how to do it," the only example of aging that our grandchildren ever see. We live our lives in front of them, endure the maladies of old age, and by our response to this suffering communicate to them how we feel about the value of life. We demonstrate the importance of human courage and resilience by overcoming difficulties and contributing and functioning even when it is not easy and convenient to do so. And thus we instill in them the courage that was once referred to as "pioneer spirit."

ào

As grandparents we are the only models of "how to do it," the only example of aging that our grandchildren ever see.

ADMITTING MORTALITY

Among students I have known at Taylor, the most common and oft-repeated shock to our students is the death of their grandparents. Many of them have this experience during their student years. They struggle deeply and have great difficulty in accepting this loss. I often wonder if they've had any conversations with their grandparents about mortality and eternity. Have these grandparents ever talked with them about the inevitability of their death? Have they said, "After I'm gone, here are the things I hold valuable. These are the goals I wanted to achieve with my life. Here's what I have in mind by leaving you some money. I want you to have my tools or my boat, or my fishing tackle, or my sewing machine because of this reason. I was not able to achieve one particular goal, but my hope has always been that you might be able to do so, and I want you to know that you have my full support." Our grandchildren need to know how we feel about them, how we feel about their life and its importance, how we feel about their responsibility to carry on the continuity of our family name and our family traditions so that their grandparents stand among that "cloud of witnesses" the book of Hebrews speaks of.

Every once in a while I meet a young man or woman who has a clear idea about all of this, quite often in the context of a family farm or a family business. The young person says to me, "My great-grandfather started this business; these were the contributions he made, then my father added to those, and now I am attempting to continue."

I have a young business friend who is the third generation in a business which has created a quality product, the standard of their industry. The competition against foreign business tempts him to cheapen the product, to do away with the standards, to sell it to someone else, make a few dollars, and get out. He feels the weight of this temptation and has told me repeatedly he would rather close the business than to produce a shoddy product in the name of his grandfather. These intergenerational traditions of excellence are an important part of the foundation of civilization.

જે

We need to keep our grandchildren close enough to us that they can observe the difficulties we go through, but understand that we do have what Peter called the blessed hope.

The Old Testament is full of stories of grandfathers bringing their sons and grandsons around their deathbed to make statements to them which cement the relationship as envisioned by the older generation. These are recorded as sacred in Scripture because they have importance.

We need to keep our grandchildren close enough to us that they can observe the difficulties we go through, sense our temperament while we're struggling, share our burdens with us—but above all, understand that we do have what Peter called the blessed hope. We believe in the resurrection of Jesus Christ from the dead. We may be a little unclear as to how these eternal things fit together, and we may not understand altogether what heaven will be like, but we have put our faith in a loving and caring God. We believe that the One who made this world and gave it meaning has prepared a place for us and we are prepared to go and be with him for all eternity. Grandchildren who have a memory of their grandparents, prepared, ready, and unafraid of death, possess a knowledge that will give strength to their lives in the future.

FACING DEATH

When a loved one dies, the family is often invited by the mortician for a private viewing of the body before the official visitation begins. When I am close to the family, I usually try to be with them at this time. The initial shock of seeing a loved one in the casket for the first time can be traumatic, and support is welcomed and useful.

One evening I was performing this function with a rather large family, with a dozen or so grandchildren present, ranging from five years of age to high school upperclassmen. The children were disconsolate, nearly hysterical. I gathered them around the body of their grandmother and had them hold hands. I asked two of the older ones to touch their grandmother's hands while we prayed together.

After the prayer I asked them how they felt. They said they were afraid to touch her and that really the body didn't seem like grandma at all. Something was missing.

I talked to them about the soul and the New Testament verse that speaks of being "absent from the body but present with the Lord." I asked them if they thought Grandma was a Christian. All agreed that she was the best Christian they had ever known. We discussed her aches and pains and what she looked like as a young woman. Gradually they constructed a narrative of their own based upon the biblical teachings on immortality and heaven. "Grandma doesn't have arthritis anymore. Now she can climb a ladder and pick apples again. I'll bet she and Grandpa are catching up on all the news. She's probably getting ready for Mom and Dad to visit her soon."

Dealing directly with death helps children face up to

the truth rather than acting like grandparents just vaporize and disappear out of our lives. Kids need to be dignified as persons and allowed to struggle with these verities of life and to be helped to fit the pieces together.

Many years ago, I was filling the pulpit for a small country church in New Paris, Indiana, during the summer months while I was a student. The pastor of the church was in the parsonage next door to the church, dying of cancer. Each Sunday before service I would go over to his home and have a prayer with him, discuss my sermon, and he would give me words of encouragement.

Over several weeks I began to feel close to him and my prayers became more fervent and caring. One Sunday I held his hand in both of mine and prayed for the service and for him. "Lord," I said, "I pray that you would heal our brother, that you would raise him up and bring him back again and help him to be well enough to preach and shepherd the flock."

While I was praying he shook my hands and interrupted my prayer. "Jay, don't pray like that," he said. "You don't seem to understand. I've spent seventy years getting ready to go to heaven, and about the time I'm ready to go, you're trying to gyp me out of it."

I related the incident in the service that followed; the congregation was delighted by the fact that what their pastor preached really worked for him. And I was grateful for a man who was willing to open his soul and share that kind of truth with me.

When we're young and vigorous and full of anticipation, with goals and plans and aspirations, we don't always think about the reality of death. We store them away in our hearts, and somehow the Holy Spirit brings them back to memory at the time we need them.

LOOKING FOR THE BLESSINGS

On another occasion I went to preach a midweek service at a little Indiana church. Somehow I arrived about an hour before the service began. I found an open door and went inside and, as I often do in strange churches, read the bulletin board, trying to figure out what the life of the church was like. I took a look at the hymnal and did a Sherlock Holmes kind of investigation to see what I was getting into.

Then I heard a man working in the back of the church. I walked back and found an elderly gentleman sweeping one of the back rooms. I introduced myself and he introduced himself as the church sexton. He told me that he was glad I was there, the time of the service and when the pastor would arrive.

As we talked further he asked me about my plans in life and about my sense of God's will for my life. I explained that I felt called to the ministry, and that I was attempting to fulfill the calling of the evangelist, going from church to church, preaching and gaining experience.

He said to me, "Well, you wouldn't have any way of knowing this, but I am the former pastor of this church. I was pastor for forty years. When I got ready for retirement, I didn't have any place to go. The congregation asked me to stay in the community. In fact, a group of men in the church helped me to get a down-payment to buy my little house. Would you like to come visit?"

I walked half a block down the street to a modest, neat little house on the edge of the highway. Obviously this was a low priced house and within his budget, because the highway had nearly taken off the front porch. Inside, however, it was wonderfully clean.

He introduced me to his wife and she offered me some tea and cookies. As we sat down I commented on the neatness of the house, and with a sense of true and sincere gratitude, he said to me, "Isn't the Lord wonderful? There's a verse in the Bible that says, 'God will not allow his servant to beg bread.' I've had such a full life; I've had a chance to preach and be a part of this congregation. I feel surrounded by love. In fact, all the people in the church feel like sons and daughters to me, and their children like my grandchildren. Look how wonderfully God's taken care of us. I just wanted you to see our home and be with us a little while, because some day you'll grow old, and you should know that God will take care of you."

They preached to me a little sermon from Matthew 6:33, "Seek ye first the Kingdom of God and His righteousness and all these things will be added unto you."

I'm sure if people came from a big city magazine or newspaper into that town and observed the modest home in which the man lived, they might analyze his life and write an article reflecting the terrible condition of the elderly clergy in our country. They could expand on the fact that he was living in a very small town, an hour or more from a hospital, with no available medical care, and paint a very bleak picture. The pastor however, didn't view it this way at all. He was looking at his blessings.

BEING REAL

Max Terhune, who filled in some of the gaps for our kids when their grandparents were absent, had a profound impact on my son Bruce, both in life and in death.

As Max grew older and got into his late eighties, he had

an aneurysm that caused symptoms much like a stroke. He became confused and found it difficult to drive. His family asked me to confront him with the dangers to himself and others in driving his car. He knew we were right, but it was a difficult blow. At last he agreed, with some frustration and anger.

When we were alone he said to me, "Jay, make me a promise that you won't let me die with tubes up my nose." I said I wasn't sure that I could keep such a promise, but I would try.

As his health deteriorated I visited him and we prayed together. Each time he reaffirmed his desire about the "tubes up his nose." I took Bruce along on the day he died. He was weak and barely able to talk, but he looked up at us and winked and said, "Thanks for keeping them from putting tubes up my nose."

Bruce and I cried and laughed as we remembered him together. He was a strong and good man, at peace with God and the world. He did not fear death and didn't want to act as if he did. "Life is real," he always said, and for him that meant "no tubes." For Max, and for us, both life and death involve courage.

ॐ

Grandparents have an opportunity to help young people get this longer view, to see mortality for what it really is, to measure things with eternity's values.

All grandparents, at some time in their lives, have an opportunity to help young people get this longer view, to see mortality for what it really is, to measure things with eternity's values. We can point to a faithful God and say, "I've lived a long life, I've had a lot of experiences, and I can tell you, you can trust God. You can believe in him; he'll take care of you."

This gift from grandparents to grandchildren is something no one else can give to them. We can't really talk about old age unless we are experiencing it, facing for ourselves the specter of death. And young people cannot live full lives without some acquaintance with and understanding of this part of human experience. As grandparents, we can gently usher our grandchildren into an understanding of death not as an end, but as a beginning—a doorway into eternity.

THIRTEEN

Providing Support

D URING VISITATION DAYS for prospective students at the University, I usually arrive early in the morning at a coffee hour where these students and their parents gather for a day of looking at the college. They ask questions, see our promotional film, and try to decide where to attend college. I do the obligatory presidential presentation, welcoming them and answering questions. I try to be available and give them a sense of who we are. There are usually grandparents with them, either accompanying the parents and children, as a kind of morale booster, or as surrogates, carrying on the role of parents.

I met a woman who was well into her seventies, dignified and attractive. She told me that her granddaughter was on campus, and I told her it was great to see grandparents attending, since these kids need all the support they can get. A look of terror came over her face, and she said, "Oh, no. I can't support her all the way! I don't have enough money to do that."

Smiling, I replied, "I understand what you're saying. I meant moral support, not financial. They need someone at their side during a day like this because it can be a frightening experience."

But the look in her eyes brought up familiar feelings in me; it seems as if I spend a lot of time these days thinking of ways to amass enough financial base to assure that all nine of our grandchildren can go to college. I know it doesn't all fall on me; they have other grandparents and concerned parents. Yet if I don't come through, I feel as if it may not happen. And I am vitally interested in their getting a good educational background—if possible, a quality Christian education.

When I viewed this grandmother's face, I realized she was thinking only in terms of financial support. She relaxed and laughed after I disarmed the situation, yet the reality hangs in our minds. How can we be the support we desire to be to our children's families, especially to our grandchildren?

REDEFINING SUPPORT

If we have the resources, we can be of great financial help to our grandchildren. But we mustn't allow the word "support" to refer only to money. Some of us, after all, don't have the financial resources to help provide for college tuition, car loans, and mortgage payments. And under certain cirumstances, providing too much financial assistance can be damaging to our grandchildren.

But the emotional and spiritual support we can give goes far beyond dollars. The grandmother of the Taylor student was doing one of the most important things we can do. She was available and present to show her interest and to give significance to her granddaughter's life.

Standing by. Over the years I have worked with thousands of young people, some from good homes, with caring parents, surrounded by love and affluence, and some from economically deprived backgrounds with few of the amenities associated with the American dream. I have worked with troubled youth in juvenile institutions, work camps, and off-the-street youth centers.

All teenagers seem somewhat prone to experimentation and testing. Some get into trouble with drugs or alcohol; some steal for the thrill, some because they can't stop, and some to make money. Many have minor scrapes with the law, mostly with alcohol or driving or both. Some get involved in crime at a serious and vicious level.

But the one thing all these kids have in common is that they usually do not recover from their problems unless there are caring people around them to provide support—standing by them, encouraging positive behavior, and affirming their love and concern for them. In short, young people need caring adults who will not give up on them. Even kids standing before the judge have a far better chance of redemption if someone—preferably a family member—is willing to stand at their side. Accompanying a child for a teacher's conference, a disciplinary hearing with a principal, or even standing with a grandchild before a judge can be difficult and threatening. But it can be vital to our loved ones.

ॐ

Kids usually do not recover from their problems unless there are caring people around them to provide support. Young people need caring adults who will not give up on them.

Being there. In some ways, we may never know how much value our "ounce of prevention" has had in a grandchild's

life. But we need to take the risk—even if we can't always
see the outcome. We can show our grandchildren that we
care. We can be there as much as possible to provide them
with a sense of value.

ॐ

*We may never know how much value our
"ounce of prevention" has had in a grandchild's life. But we need to take the risk—
even if we can't always see the outcome.*

There is a direct correlation between the number of
people who care for us and our ability to withstand, overcome, cope, and recover. A tearful high school senior
poured out his feelings, saying, "I owe everything to my
grandma. She took care of my brother and me after my
mother left. We raised birds and had fun watching them
hatch and grow up. She taught me to play chess and took
me to the zoo. We flew kites; she took me to see the fire-
works and never missed a Little League game. I know she
really wasn't that interested in all of these things, but she
did it for me. She really cares about me."

This young man had lost his father through divorce,
then his mother deserted him to his grandmother's care.
He might have made it without his grandmother. Perhaps
a social agency or a Christian organization would have
intervened. But without his grandmother's care, he might
have ended up as another heartbreaking statistic.

Communication. Another young girl told me that she had
been forced to care for her little sister because her mother
was mentally ill with an obsessive/compulsive disorder. The

woman was afraid to clean the house or touch anyone or anything, including the telephone, and she washed her hands several dozen times a day.

The girl, physically abused by her father, sought help from the church. She and her sister were living with caring people from the church and she told me that the letters she received from her grandmother in Texas were her greatest sense of joy. Her grandmother understood and cared and wanted to know about what was going on at school—about her grades, her flute, her faith, her youth group. She said, "My grandma's letters are everything to me. I can be honest with her and share my feelings and she understands."

The grandmother would probably confess a feeling of helplessness and despair, feeling that her letters and prayers were ineffective. But these seemingly small gestures *are* important—sometimes they can mean the difference between survival and surrender.

One couple wrote in some detail, expressing the problems in their family and the fact that they had been removed by both relocation and distance from their grandchildren. They were making cassette tape recordings to send to the grandchildren each month, telling them of their love and support, and the two of them were reading books onto the tapes so that the grandchildren could hear their voices and follow along as they read.

"This is about all we can do under the circumstances," they said. "But at least it's something." I think it's quite a lot, and they will find it was important in the long run.

Listening. Two recent letters illustrate a grandchild's perspective. One wrote, "My grandfather was curious about everything in life. He was always asking questions rather than talking all the time. He was truly a good listener. I guess he made me feel important, like I had something to say."

Another said, "My grandmother was a teacher and I lived with her. I would help her grade papers and file for her. She gave me responsibility, and I was flattered. She exposed me to music and the finer things of life. She is always interested in what I do, and even now that I have my own family, she comes to church to hear my choir perform. She's my greatest inspiration and support. I don't know what I'll do without her."

The grandmother who protested, "Oh, no, I can't support her all the way!" was right in one way. But in other ways she was doing a wonderful job of support, and the first school bill hadn't even arrived.

Phone calls, letters, attending school functions, going places together, and developing our listening skills—none of these cost money, but they are important ways of showing support.

Sharing the pain. I once visited an African village where the custom was that whenever any family faced a crisis, the elders of the village sat around the yard in front of the house and, without saying anything, were there and available to share the burden. I was told that this was an ancient custom that is never broken. No member of the village was ever allowed to suffer without everyone sharing in their distress. Perhaps this is what Jesus meant when he spoke of "bearing one another's burdens and thus fulfilling the law of Christ."

We can do that for our families—simply be there to acknowledge and share the pain. One kind of support that is desperately needed but costs no money is being a sounding board to our adult children who are parenting.

We do not need to give advice primarily, but simply the quiet knowledge that we are there. We are willing to listen, to clarify, but mostly to be.

THE LITTLE EXTRAS

We can also provide other kinds of intermediate help—short of paying for college. Many grandparents worry about the fact that kids today seem to have so much, that "we are spoiling them by giving them too much. After all, aren't they victims of the abundance of this culture?" Surely few of our grandchildren need one more plastic toy or something with another battery. They can be indulged and receive too much. But there are areas that are quite important, areas we can supplement.

Most of us remember the days when our children were young and we were struggling to support our families. Just keeping them in the basics—clothing, shoes, school supplies, insurance—can be a real burden on most young families.

All my life, for example, I've struggled with dental problems because my parents simply could not afford a dentist when I was young. Some children no longer face this problem today because of fluoride and insurance plans, but among the poor it is still a major problem. Dental work tells a lot about how much discretionary income a family has. A little boost by grandparents in these discretionary areas can make a great deal of difference even if it is not appreciated at the time.

As grandparents, we might want to think about these little extras we can provide to our children's families, such as dental work, if they don't have an insurance package that covers it.

Janie has decided that as people grow older, almost all of them wish they had had some kind of musical background. Therefore, one of our goals is to put a piano into each of our children's homes. Music lessons fall into the same category. We can offer a piano and music lessons for a year or two for each of the grandchildren. Together we feel a sense of great joy that we are able to provide this modest luxury for them. Perhaps not all grandparents are able to do this, but in our case this is one of those little boosts we can give to our grandchildren.

We feel the same way about orthodontists. People can live without orthodontic work—indeed, most of our generation did live without it. Only the rich kids in my class in high school had braces. Now braces are commonplace, and the benefits—both socially and physically—are worth the investment. If we can provide this extra support when needed, it will have important social consequences.

One grandmother tells me that she is rather tired of being a babysitter, but she's decided that it is an investment in her kids' marriages. If they are going out together to spend quality time, she'll babysit. If it's for another reason, she might decline.

Another category of "extras" is special books—such as encyclopedias—that parents might not be able to afford, but having them in the home has value. Schools have encyclopedias and children's books, but when it's possible for grandparents to provide these supplements for the home, they add lasting value and greatly enrich and enhance the young person's life. If I had the choice as a grandparent whether to provide an encyclopedia or a Nintendo, I wouldn't hesitate to choose the encyclopedia. They'll probably get the Nintendo anyway, but the encyclopedia might fall by the wayside.

Beyond these small rewards, grandparents can provide

travel and other life experiences our grandchildren wouldn't necessarily have. If we have the financial resources we can take them to concerts, to plays, to places they wouldn't see unless Grandma and Grandpa provided the experience.

ESTATE PLANNING

Beyond the *physical* resources we can provide for our grandchildren, we need to consider a deeper level of provision, one that extends beyond our own lifetime. The concept of estate planning may sound a bit foreboding to some. Isn't an estate something only wealthy people have, and isn't that a little beyond ordinary people? Actually, everyone who owns anything has an estate. We may have just a few dollars in our pockets when we die, or some leftover clothing, an old shotgun. We might own a house or a car. In most cases, we own a great deal more. Everyone has an estate; we all leave something behind when we die.

With proper planning, we can do much more for our children and grandchildren than we think we can. Each family must work out the details for themselves, but I hold the personal opinion that it is not greatly helpful to leave our children money. If we have helped them grow up and become established in a home and have provided supplemental helps along the way, by the time they get their inheritance from us, they are already established and probably don't need the money.

But if we as grandparents have the foresight to provide—through insurance, savings, or investments of some kind—resources that can be used for the education of the grandchildren, we can perform a lasting and valuable life service. Unquestionably, people who have had the advantage of more education tend to do better in this society than those who have less. Undereducated and under-prepared individuals are usually relegated to lower-paying positions. In the main, those who have more education will earn in a lifetime a good deal more money (about triple the amount) than those who have not had the advantage of education.

An investment in education is an investment in future generations that we may never see. Helping our grand-children go to college provides a wonderful service to them and to our progeny as long as our family survives.

Once we sit down with a financial counselor and think through how to maximize our resources to provide the greatest help possible for the future, we begin to get a vision of the joy in lasting ministry. Through estate planning, we can provide for the church of Jesus Christ, for the things that are close to the heart of God, such as mission societies and other Christian institutions as well.

Someone has said that "Charity begins at home." Scripture teaches us to be good stewards of our resources and to care for our families so that we are not a burden on the rest of society. I believe it's possible for grandparents to make a great difference in the future of our grand-children, of the church, and of the world.

૨૭

Scripture teaches us to be good stewards of our resources and to care for our families so that we are not a burden on the rest of society.

Much of what we do in life falls into the category of what "moth and rust corrupts." Investment in our grandchildren and in Christian ministry efforts will last forever. We really can "lay up treasures in heaven." We can invest our love, our support, our values, and our finances in our grandchildren, so that they will bear fruit for generations to come.

Other Books of Interest by Servant Publications

Unstuck

Carolyn Koons

Carolyn Koons presents fascinating new insights into human development which reveal that adults, no matter what their age, have an immense capacity to grow.

Unstuck calls readers to a profound psychological and spiritual awakening which will give them permission to change and grow. For all of us who are living longer and staying healthier, this is the guide to help us through those challenging life passages, which can lead to greater spiritual depth and deeper life satisfaction.

$16.99

Family Is *Still* a Great Idea

H. Norman Wright

Norman Wright affirms the family as the well-spring of strength and stability in our lives. With all the discussion of how the "dysfunctional family" can be the source of our deepest sorrows, *Family Is Still a Great Idea* asserts that even our imperfect family has the potential of being the source of our greatest joys. **$16.99**

Available at your Christian bookstore or from:
**Servant Publications • Dept. 209 • P.O. Box 7455
Ann Arbor, Michigan 48107**
Please include payment plus $1.25 per book
for postage and handling.
*Send for our FREE catalog of Christian
books, music, and cassettes.*